FANHOOD TO MANHOOD

SHOCK THERAPY FOR THE RECOVERING SPORTS FANATIC

TOMMY KNOXVILLE

Fanhood to Manhood:
Shock Therapy for the Recovering Sports Fanatic

© 2019, Notaed Press
All Rights Reserved

All quotes and citations included in accordance with the fair use provisions of the Copyright Act of 1976 and subsequent case law.

Audiobook ISBN: 978-1-951677-09-1
eBook ISBN: 978-0-9892542-8-1
Paperback ISBN: 978-0-9892542-7-4
Hardcover ISBN: 978-1-951677-03-9

Cover by Paula Ambrosio of
paulambrosio.com

Published by Notaed Press

For the sports fan

who's seen enough.

Contents

one I Get It 1

Part I: Fanhood

two The Drummer Boy Incident 15

three The Battle of New Orleans 25

four Ten Miles from Mexico 33

five Redemption 41

six Wyoming 49

seven The Awakening 53

Part II: Puberty

eight The Talk 63

nine Fan Brainwashing 101 71

ten The Purge 97

eleven Taking Stock 103

twelve All About the Benjamins 109

thirteen Bring It On! 119

fourteen Freud Said *What?* 129

Part III: Manhood

fifteen What, Then? 139

sixteen Midlife Crisis MMA 145

seventeen The Formula 157

eighteen Kenny Kool-Aids 175

nineteen But, But, But... Jack Nicholson 183

twenty But, But, But...
I'm Too Fat, Broke, Busy 187

twenty-one But, But, But...
It's My Outlet 193

twenty-two Return to Neyland 205

Extras

More Books by Tommy Knoxville 222

Recommended Reads 226

Acknowledgements 233

Audiobooks Plug 239

Chapter 1
I Get It

If we want it bad enough, if we yell loud enough, *if we concentrate hard enough,* maybe we'll give our boys the edge they need. Regardless, we're all in. Seeing through their eyes, feeling through their muscles, we risk defeat alongside them, and the payoff is an experience bordering on the religious.

The team affirms who we are. Their tradition = our tradition. Their reputation = our reputation. Their record = our record. Let it be known through our clothes, our ringtone, our Facebook posts: we are true fans *for life.* Why?

It's a tribe thing. The passing stranger sees our team gear, we see his – a knowing nod affirms our shared devotion. Who cares how he votes or where he goes to church? Supporting the same team means we've got his back and he's got ours.

It's a family thing. The team's how we connect with our nephew at Thanksgiving, the way we open and close phone calls with Dad. Initiated by a mentor, we vow to do our part to recruit the next generation. We buy our newborns team-themed onesies, sing them fight-song lullabies, joke how Coach can use them once they're grown. We share our excitement, our passion, give them every opportunity to follow in our diehard footsteps.

Ah, and the games themselves. The anticipation, the triumph, the group euphoria! *That's* the high we chase. *That's* the thrill that vindicates our loyalty. *That's* why we're fans.

Game time's also our chance to vent – *really* vent – and vent without getting fired, jailed or divorced (usually). The opposition, their fans, the refs become stand-ins for our boss or our ex, or simply for life not going as planned. Anonymous and emboldened, we can let loose, jeer the enemy in unison, the constraining rules of polite society suspended, if only for a few hours.

And even when we lose, at least we lose together. There's always next year. In the meantime we console one another with tales of past seasons' glory, and jointly fantasize the glories to come.

In other words, *I get it.* Being a sports fan has an understandable allure. It serves a social and personal purpose. *It feeds deep needs.*

However, there's a dark side.

When cheering for a team causes more anxiety than joy, when it affects how we show up for those we love, when it becomes an excuse for destructive behavior (binge spending, binge drinking, binge raging), when our obsession with the team's journey comes at the expense of our own journey – that's when an innocent hobby has turned toxic.

Once upon a time, this was me. My mood, my esteem and my testosterone levels depended on the athletic performance of strangers. (Your testosterone levels, too, says science –

see chapter 21.) I'd celebrate when they won and pout when they lost, sometimes for weeks at a time. Immersed in the delusion that their games had something to do with me, some of my highest thrills and deepest satisfaction came through my team. (Sound familiar?)

While I chose this life, I didn't get it by accident. A billion-dollar industry had been quietly partnering with research psychologists to make me watch more, care more, spend more. Whatever it took to boost my "Psychological Commitment to Team" score (yes, that's a thing), to move me up the "Fan Involvement Ladder" (from suspect to customer to raving fan), to ensure I frequently "BIRGed" (Basked In Reflective Glory) and seldom "CORFed" (Cut Off Reflective Failure) – their marketers had no qualms against doing it.[1]

Targeting me (and you) from a young age, they've tried to blur memories of the team with memories of family, to link their revenue source to our home and culture, all while constantly reinforcing the myth that being a crazed fan is normal, healthy, manly.

Today, five years clean, whether my old team wins or loses is of little concern. No longer beholden to the scam, I do my own thing, find satisfaction and excitement through my own adventures, and am happier for it.

---

[1] Yes, sports fan psychologists are real, and your team's marketing department really has been conspiring with them. Good news: we're about to pull back the curtain, and understanding their propaganda will make it easier to resist.

Rehab wasn't easy, especially in our sports-crazed culture. But the core realization that made it possible was this: sports teams are mere businesses, fans are mere customers, and life's too short to spend it a glorified cheerleader.

Some will find comparing fans to cheerleaders sexist. More than once I was advised to drop the analogy. "People will think you're a chauvinist pig. What about female fans?"

Right or wrong, seeing fanhood as cheerleading and team gear as a cheerleading skirt was essential to my recovery. It heightened my disdain and made vivid what a sissified waste fanhood can be.

As you'll soon see, I had to hit rock bottom to appreciate how destructive my obsession had become. And I needed to disparage it as harshly as I could to make my liberation permanent.

So offensive or not, you're getting the same. And it's especially important that you get it from me when everyone else seems content to perpetuate the industry's myth:

> "It's about tradition, loyalty, hard-won pride. It's a tribe thing, a primal thing, embedded in our DNA. The struggle, the triumph, the sacrifice and glory – *being a sports fan is part of what it means to be a real man.*"

Bullshit.

Real men don't revolve their lives around the athletic performance of strangers. They don't prance about in other men's jerseys, or waste their weekends obsessing over a game they're not even playing. They find satisfaction and pride in *their* accomplishments – live *their* lives, not pretend lives with pretend connections to artificial stars in a made-up spectacle.

The harsh truth is that the life of the rabid sports fan (which was me for many years) is a pathetic waste. But the glorious hope is that escape is possible, and you're holding the how-to manual.

Born in different places, I might have been a fan of your team, or you of mine. But my bet is that whether you were sucked into following American football, Argentinian fútbol or Australian rugby, the themes – communal pride, emotional gambling, deepening addiction during a time of strife – are universal. And not only am I betting on common causes, I'm betting on a common cure.

As you read the story of my degeneration into toxic fanaticism in *Part I: Fanhood,* consider parallels in your own journey. We may not share the same sport or the same team. But we do share the same basic needs, and I'm betting the sports industry manipulated yours in a similar way.

As you absorb the tough love of *Part II: Puberty,* remember why you're here. One too many weekends wasted? A brokenhearted family member? A sense that the squealing and whining are beneath you? Whatever the case, don't be too hard on yourself, and know that better days are ahead.

And as you begin your new, triumphant chapter with *Part III:*

Manhood, remain strong. Know that your internal "bad wolf" will try to derail your recovery *(Turn the game on... Just check the score... You know you wanna).* "Kenny Kool-Aids" will emerge with free tickets and promises of championships just around the corner *(It's our year – I can feel it!).* Resist. Remain vigilant. And begin steeling your will now, for relapse triggers will appear from within, as well as from without, guaranteed.

Fanhood may have served you at one time. But now is the time to put down the pom-poms and throw away that frilly pink skirt.

Welcome to the path of fanhood to manhood.

Part I

Fanhood

Chapter 2
The Drummer Boy Incident

In the fall of 2014, the University of Tennessee Volunteer football team faced the Florida Gators under the cloud of a nine-year losing streak. For almost a decade the Vol faithful had believed this would be the year their loyalty would finally be rewarded. And for almost a decade, they had been wrong.

But in 2014 the optimism was justified. The Vols had more talent, more experience, and the home field advantage: *Neyland Stadium* – a venue as loud and intimidating as any in the country.

More than 100,000 fans strong, their deafening roar caused opposing teams' linemen to false start, quarterbacks to stutter, and waterboys to wet their pants.

But for this special occasion, a visual disruption tactic was added. Instructions went out the week of the game that fans were to color-coordinate based on seating.

> "If your ticket is in section A-1, wear orange. Section, A-2: white. B-1: orange. Repeat. If in doubt, consult *#CheckerNeyland* online."

The result was an extension of the stadium's iconic checkerboard end zones all the way through the upper decks. A glorious backdrop for the victory to come, the repeating pattern promised to confuse Florida's receivers *(Which way do I run?!),* and when combined with the precise frequency of crowd noise, timed at *just* the right moment, give their placekicker a seizure.

As Southeastern Conference battles often do, the game proved a defensive chess match. After a scoreless first quarter Tennessee went up 3-0 with a field goal. Then another extended our lead to 6-0 before the half. At the end of the third quarter the mighty Vols were leading nine to nothing.

Just 15 minutes more and the miserable streak would be over. Ten years of disappointment, a stadium overflowing with anticipation, on the cusp of release. Nine to nothing wouldn't be as satisfying as a double-digit blowout. But we'd take a win any way we could get it.

Then in the final quarter, having held back the Gator onslaught for 45 minutes of play, our defense blinked. Florida scored a touchdown. The extra point narrowed our lead to two.

While nonideal, this was acceptable. After nine losses in a row, a two-point win wouldn't be the shutout we had hoped for. But a two-point win would still be a win.

Then Florida scored a field goal of their own, taking the lead for the first time: 10 to 9.

Late in the 4th and desperate to score, the Vols had the ball and were driving. Slowly, we made it across midfield with less than two minutes left.

This would be the championship run, the last-minute victory that fans would relish for years to come. "Remember back in 2014 when we hit that sideline bomb in the final seconds? Touchdown, Big Orange!" Nothing wrong with a little suspense, so long as all ended well.

Our Vols were probably just toying with the Gators – offering a glimmer of hope before sending the team and their fans south with daggers through their reptile hearts. We'd be sure to sing them a consoling favorite as they made their way out of the stadium:

> "It's great, to be, a Tennessee Vol;
> I said it's great, to be, a Tennessee Vol!"

Maybe today would mark the

beginning of a winning streak of our own? We were primed to celebrate and ready to sing.

But when a Volunteer pass sailed into the hands of a Gator defender, the fantasy came crashing down. Without enough timeouts to force a punt, Florida ran out the clock still ahead by a single point.

There was no last-minute Hail Mary, no slow-motion sprint to the end zone, no Big Orange glory to relive the next morning at church. Our stadium noise, our color-coordinated seating (we'd provided a glorious backdrop alright... for another loss...), our faith that *this* was the year – all ultimately impotent.

The team, the crowd, the entire

Vol nation realized that despite our best efforts, we'd just lost to our most hated rival for an entire decade.

An entire decade! How could this happen... *again!?* Was there a fan who hadn't yelled loudly enough? Who hadn't concentrated intently enough? Whose faith wasn't strong enough?

Florida's class act of a coach, Will Muschamp (who would be fired later that season), gleefully told a sideline reporter, "It's great to see all these people out here gettin' disappointed – *I love it."*

The Florida band, perhaps following Muschamp's lead, decided to send the brokenhearted home with one last jab. They raised their instruments high and played "Rocky Top," our fight song, in our stadium, punctuating what everyone already knew – that the Gators effectively *owned* our Vols, as well as our stadium.

> *"Rocky Top, you'll always be, home sweet home to me… Good old Rocky Top (whoo!)… Rocky Top, Tennessee…"*

As he willed himself out of his seat and towards the exit, a dejected Vol fan was coming to terms with the year of loathing ahead. The familiar sting, the shame, the helplessness.

Demoralized and angry, he lashed out, elbowing his way through pockets of Gator fans.

"Out of the way… *Out of the way!*"

Just outside the stadium, he

barged west along Tee Martin Drive. Ahead he could see the Florida band marching toward their bus, beaming with smugness.

On a collision course, he didn't slow. And when he made it to the band that had just played *his* team's fight song, in *his* stadium, he tantrumed right through the middle of their formation.

"Out of the way... *Out of the way...*"

A Florida drummer took offense.

"No, *you* get out of the way."

The man snapped.

"I'll shove those drumsticks *up your ass!*"

The never-ending losses had hurt. And we'd have to wait yet another year for our chance to break the streak.

But how could a grown man get *that* upset over a game he wasn't even playing? Upset enough to elbow through groups of strangers? Upset enough to threaten some poor college drummer?

I'm ashamed to admit that grown man was me.

How did an otherwise respectable professional, a husband and father, allow himself to get *that* wrapped up, *that* mad?

My breakdown was the crescendo of a toxic fanaticism that had been festering for almost 30 years.

Chapter 3
The Battle of New Orleans

Let's briefly rewind to New Year's Day, 1986.

Eight-year-old me and my five-year-old sister lie on sleeping bags on the living room floor, Mom and Dad behind us on the couch. The horses and chickens fed early, all eyes are on the TV, for it's football time in Tennessee.

With almost a month to anticipate the biggest matchup in memory, the entire state is abuzz. The #8 Vols are fresh off their first Southeastern Conference championship in 16 years and are set to play #2 Miami in the New Orleans Sugar Bowl.

On site 600 miles south at the Superdome, Vol fans outnumber Miami fans two to one. My Aunt Dot is among them. When the cameras pan the crowd, my sister tries to catch a glimpse.

"I think I see her!"

The fans in orange and white were ready for an upset victory, but the national analysts considered that to be a very unlikely outcome. "These scrubs from Knoxville? Beat the perennially powerful Hurricanes – the same Hurricanes with Heisman Trophy-winning quarterback Vinnie Testaverde? Not a chance."

Back then, the bowls determined the national champion, and Miami was actually in the running. With a regular season win over #3 Oklahoma, ABC Sports announcers Frank Broyles and Keith Jackson argued whether the winner of Oklahoma's bowl game against #1 Penn State or Miami should be declared the national champion. After all, the fact that Miami would beat Tennessee was a foregone conclusion.

> Broyles: "If Penn State loses, Miami will be the national champion…"
>
> Jackson: "Do you think Tennessee, with its defense now, can manifest some pressure on Testaverde?"
>
> Broyles: "Oklahoma could not, Keith. I think for Tennessee to have any chance in this ballgame, they've got to roll the dice… They hope to confuse Testaverde, who I

think may be the best college passer we've seen in a long, long time."

Their analysis made it clear that no one outside the Volunteer state gave our boys a fighting chance. Tennessee fans took this lack of respect personally. In fact, more than 30 years later, many still haven't forgotten. If you find the broadcast on YouTube, there's a comment from a "Jack Buck" that perfectly captures the sentiment.

> "I swear, if Tennessee played the Al Qaeda Child Killers, [announcer] Keith Jackson would be for the Child Killers. He hated Tennessee, he hated Peyton Manning, he hated everything but Alabama."

That's today. But back on New Year's Day 1986, win or lose, Coach

Johnny Majors was determined to ensure his Vols would never be overlooked again. His pre-game locker room speech turned the team's underdog status into a weapon (or if you've seen *The Waterboy*, into "tackling fuel").

> "They don't have any respect for you. Make them remember you for as long as they live – for the way you hit, the way you knock them down downfield, the way you hustle."

The team apparently listened. Miami scored a touchdown in the opening quarter, but never again.

What about their Heisman Trophy-winning quarterback? As the New York Times described it:

"The Tennessee defense sacked Testaverde seven times and pressured him on almost every passing play... forced him into three fumbles... intercepted Testaverde three times and his replacement once."

Our team, our state, our culture vindicated, my family cheered with families all over Tennessee as our Vols stunned the so-called "experts" and won what would become known locally as the "Battle of New Orleans." The final score: 35 to 7.

I thought to myself, "Man, I'd have given anything to be there – to see the Vols win in person like Aunt Dot."

The following year my dad surprised me with tickets to the UT-California game. I still remember how far away we had to park (a mile seems further when you're ten), how loud the crowd was, and how proud Dad seemed to be for taking me.

Our Vols didn't disappoint. Cal's Golden Bears went down quietly, and the ticket stubs and pom-poms from my first game (a 38-to-12 Big Orange win) hung on my bedroom wall for the remainder of my childhood.

The seeds of fanhood planted early, my first game mementoes would be ever-present reminders that whatever else happened, I was a Vol for life.

Chapter 4
Ten Miles from Mexico

Fast forward to 1997. I'm at Laughlin Air Force Base, a pilot training station in the Texas desert, charged with maintaining air traffic control tower radios.

Much of the lone star state is beautiful. But two and a half hours southwest of San Antonio, I might as well have been on the moon.

> Grass? What's grass? (Do you mean *cactus?*) What are these *"trees"* you speak of? (Do mesquite bushes count?) And in your land, the earth is tall in some

places, and short in others? It is not flat? Very odd, this "Tennessee."

That the blazing furnace called summer produced a "dry" heat was little consolation for those of us in battle dress uniforms and combat boots. The air conditioner in the truck we drove to and from the receiver site could hardly keep up.[2] But it was better than the alternative. Rolling down the window felt like someone was shooting you in the face with a hair dryer.

In short, the lush Appalachian foothills I'd taken for granted as a kid –

---

[2] The receiver site was a one-roomed building beside the landing strip that housed dozens of radio receivers (too many to fit in the tower), each dedicated to a specific frequency. Rather a plumbed toilet or a port-a-potty, Uncle Sam saw fit to bless the receiver site with an incinerator commode that would literally burn your poop. The protocol: do your business, hit flush, RUN.

I learned to appreciate them. Fast. And I wasn't alone. Airmen from all over the country endorsed Laughlin's unofficial motto: "Ten miles from Mexico, ten feet from hell."

Homesick in the age before webcams, every Saturday during football season I was somewhere in front of a TV. I might have been stuck in the desert. But if I sat close enough to the screen, for a few hours, I was back home.

The sea of orange pouring into the stadium. The Pride of the Southland Marching Band. Rocky Top. I can still hear the trumpets of CBS's militaristic SEC matchup music (the same militaristic SEC matchup music they play today):

> "Daaah duh da duuuh, duh du da duuh... *Du da da dah!*"

For a young Airman, the Vols weren't only a tie to my desperately-missed home, they were a source of self-esteem.

There's always a pecking order at work: Sally, Sammy, Tammy, *then* Fred. In civilian life, you can escape it at the end of the workday. Sally and Fred go their separate ways, and Fred gets a respite. However, as any veteran can attest, this is not the case in the military.

There are plenty of good things about joining the service. It can be an escape from bad influences, an opportunity to learn a trade or mature before college, a chance to make lifelong friends, to see the world, or to simply serve your country. But one downside is that the workplace pecking order isn't exclusive to the workplace. If you're Fred at work, you're Fred everywhere, for your rank is sewn onto your shirt and everyone lives in the same fenced-in town. There is no escape.

That asshole from work is at the gym. He's at the bowling alley, the laundromat, the cafeteria. (This has to be a thousand times worse in the Navy, trapped on a freaking boat...)

And it's not only the asshole from *your* work, it's assholes from *everybody's* work, some of whom think it's their job to reassert their rank wherever you go. They're assholes, you're a lower rank – the military can be a prick's paradise.

But my Vols had *Peyton Freaking Manning!* He was breaking passing records and wowing the national media. The same experts who wouldn't give us a chance against Miami in '86 suddenly couldn't kiss our asses hard enough in '96. So I ran with it.

> "Peyton plays for *my* team, in *my* state, at *my* stadium."

I flew University of Tennessee flags on my car, decorated the Christmas tree in my dorm with orange lights, and changed into Vol gear as soon as I got off duty. Air Force camouflage off, Volunteer orange on.

This was pretty normal back home. People never questioned why you were wearing such an odd color. But on base, constantly in orange garb paired with a country drawl, I became the hillbilly with odd fashion sense.

Fixing radios for the Air Force was a fantastic way to spend my late teens and early twenties. God knows my stateside, peacetime service was cushy. To all the combat vets, thank you for yours.

But living in the desert at the bottom of the chain of command tended to suck, and that suckage made me extra vulnerable to sports fanaticism. (Self-reflection time: did your own fanaticism take hold during a similar period?)

While I liked the Vols beforehand, it was during my time in the military that they became an unhealthy obsession. The team came to represent the best of all I had left back home, and tying my pride to the outcome of their games (which was usually positive during the Manning era) entwined the University of

Tennessee Athletic Department with my very identity.

Having seen one too many cacti (and pricked one too many times), I petitioned my commanding officer to transfer to the Tennessee Air National Guard. And in the summer of 1998, I flew home whistling Rocky Top.

Chapter 5
Redemption

Despite that Sugar Bowl upset win over Miami and a handful of SEC championships, the Vols were always two steps away from true greatness. Peyton had owned Bama, which felt great after the misery of the late '80s ("BUCK FAMA" bumper stickers were not uncommon during that time). But for all his divine athleticism, Peyton never beat the Florida Gators.

I'd stuck with the team regardless, a Vol for life. My favorite t-shirt said it all: "I Bleed Orange and White!"

But when I returned from Texas in '98, even though Manning had just left for the NFL, it was magical – like I (along with thousands of other loyal fans) was finally being rewarded.

Instead of the "rebuilding" year everyone had braced for, it proved a season of drama and victory followed by drama and victory: a pass interference call in the opener against Syracuse that led to a game-saving field goal, Arkansas's quarterback fortuitously fumbling (all by his lonesome) when the game was surely lost (allowing running back Travis "Cheese" Henry to pound downfield for the win), a sideline bomb against Florida State in the national championship (that's right, *my* Vols in the *National Freaking Championship!*).

But the memory that outshines the rest: after five annual losses (a shameful streak preceding the decade of losses to come), the top-10 Vols had a fighting chance to beat top-10 Florida.

The Gators had shut down our beloved Peyton, and it was time for revenge. There was no way I was missing it. I scrounged together $150 for a scalped ticket in the southern end zone upper deck, three rows beneath where the jumbotron sits today (that's right, $150 for a single nosebleed ticket in 1998).

High school buddy and roommate, Robert (another rabid fan who'd later name his firstborn Neyland after the legendary coach) was in.

A back-and-forth defensive grinder, neither team could establish dominance. And at the end of regulation we were tied 17 to 17.

Robert and I had never seen a college game go into overtime – the rule had only been around for two seasons. Word passed quickly through the crowd that unlike in the pros, college overtime gives each team the ball on the 25-yard line and a chance to score. If after one rotation a team is leading, they win. If the score is still even, another overtime ensues.

The Vols got the ball first. We couldn't reach the end zone, and so opted for a field goal to go up 20-17.

Now Florida's turn, they could win with a touchdown. But UT linebacker Al Wilson went into beast mode and said no.

When 3rd down became 4th, the Gators needed to match the Vols' field goal to tie the game and force a second overtime.

I once weathered a severe hail storm (some claimed it was a tornado) in an old farmhouse. As my wife and I huddled in the bathroom with our dogs, it peeled the paint off the siding and laid siege to the tin roof. Can you imagine how loud that must have been?

That's how loud Neyland Stadium was as Florida's kicker lined up for the game-tying attempt. If he hits it, we go to a second overtime and risk losing. If he misses, game over – Vols (finally) win.

The fans were in agreement – let's end this *now*. Tornado-grade stadium noise, *commence.*

Five years of thwarted hope, five years of pent up frustration, all brought to bear on one play. Correction: on one *player*.

With the deafening roar in the background, here's how the late, great Vol sportscaster John Ward called it:

> "The snap... The kick is in the air, and the kick this time is... *NO – SIR – REE... NO – SIR – REE...* **Final Score**: Tennessee **20**, Florida **17**. *Pandemonium reigns."*

Pandemonium was a good word for it. Thousands of vindicated (many inebriated) fans jumping, hollering, and taunting anyone wearing blue with that full-armed "chomp" clap Gator fans hold so dear.

Orange-and-white Tasmanian devils whirl-winding onto the field, dismantling the goal posts (which were mere stumps by the time Robert and I got down there), wildly embracing, pillaging souvenirs.

I still have a clump of orange grass commandeered from the end zone (one of the few mementoes to survive "the purge" we'll soon talk about). From the looks of the field that night, lots of Vol fans do.

The chaos spilling into the streets, a group of fans paraded down Cumberland Avenue with a goal post, where legend has it, they threw it into the Tennessee River. Too many and too wild to contain, campus police wisely allowed the celebration (borderline riot) to run its course.

It still gives me goosebumps (even today, five years on the recovery side of fanhood). An unforgettable night, an unforgettable season, the Vols went undefeated the year I returned home from the Air Force: 13 wins, 0 losses.

We couldn't win the big one with the great Peyton Manning. But somehow we were all rewarded for our loyalty the year after he left for the NFL with our first win over Florida in 5 years, and our first national championship in over 30.

And as UT's reputation as a football powerhouse swelled, so did my addiction.

Chapter 6
Wyoming

Fast forward a decade. I'm holding my six-month-old firstborn in one hand and tickets to the 2008 Wyoming game in the other.

Sane fathers keep their babies indoors in November, and my wife is (intelligently) encouraging me to reconsider. But I wanted his fanaticism to match mine, and this would lay the foundation.

"Six months is old enough for my boy's first blowout win. Just bundle him up. Go Vols!"

The setup was the opposite of the '86 Sugar Bowl. This time the Vols were the heavy favorite.

As the Associated Press put it, "Wyoming came in a nearly four-touchdown underdog, the lowest-scoring team in major college football, ranked 111th in total offense and languishing near the bottom of the Mountain West Conference."

Needless to say, for an SEC heavyweight like Tennessee, the Cowboys were not a threat. And while a lopsided win might lack dramatic thrills, at least my baby boy would get initiated into the Vol family in style. Or so I thought...

While expected to beat lowly Wyoming, the once-great Vols had tumbled. They'd been splitting wins with the Gator menace, even winning three of four from '01 through '04. But no longer in the running for SEC championships, let alone national championships, their overall record wasn't living up to fans' expectations.

A vocal sect was sure that Head Coach Phillip Fulmer, who'd brought us the national championship in '98, was to blame, and their calls for his resignation were increasingly louder.

If fans could have predicted the misery to come under coaches Kiffin, Dooley and Jones (and probably Pruitt, who's new and not off to a promising start [2021 update: Pruitt was just fired... *yikes*...]), they might have given Fulmer another chance. But the Monday before that fateful Wyoming game, the university's athletic director announced

Fulmer was being pushed out and would officially step down at the end of the season. (A decade later, Fulmer would return as UT's athletic director himself. How's that for a dish served cold?)

The team did not respond well. To the shock of everyone, probably including the Cowboy players, Wyoming won and my son's first game at Neyland Stadium was a complete bust.

It hurt at the time, but looking back, it was actually a blessing.

Chapter 7
The Awakening

While my own dad had taken me to my first Vols game when I was 10 (and to see Michael Jordan and the Bulls in an exhibition game when I was 14), he was never crazy about any sports team. He was fond of the Celtics' Larry Bird. But I can't remember him getting upset over a game or putting team stickers on our Clark Griswold station wagon – not even once.

Rather than attaching his happiness to the fortune of athletic strangers, he had a competitive outlet of his own – showing horses.

While teenage strangers in orange were losing to teenage strangers in crimson every October (the third Saturday traditionally reserved for the UT-Bama game), Dad was adding trophies and ribbons to the barn's tack room display. Through his upkeep of the farm, training and competing on "Pepper," a musclebound black stallion who brought us an Amateur World Grand Championship in 1978, he (and Mom, who also competed) provided an example of how to get your kicks directly – through personal challenge, adventure and growth.

He didn't cheer for others. Others cheered for him.

My kids, on the other hand, had the opposite experience – a front row ticket to the shameful underbelly of sports fanaticism – an irate, irritable, sullen dad, complete with the shouting, pouting, and powerless attachment to events over which I had no control.

Hyping whatever matchup the Vols happened to be playing days in advance, come game time I'd don an old #16 jersey, shove pom-poms in their hands, turn the TV up as loud as it would go and proceed to model various forms of immature foolishness.

A prime example of how *not* to live an authentic, meaningful life, by the time I offered that Florida drummer a creative enema in 2014 (sorry dude, existential meltdown) I had consumed hundreds of hours of games, and spent thousands of hours listening to sports talk, reading articles, polishing team memorabilia – reinforcing precisely how my kids *shouldn't* spend their limited time on this wondrous planet.

Team bibs, team pacifiers, team stickers on their baby swings – the indoctrination unfortunately worked. Though they rebounded from losses more easily, my kids learned to love the players, to hate their rivals, and accepted the team's identity as part of our own. (As a toddler, our oldest would spontaneously sing Rocky Top at Walmart. At the time, this made me proud.)

Eight years after the Wyoming loss, it took that tenth-in-a-row loss against Florida followed by a public meltdown for me to realize how absorbed I had become, and how much of a waste sports fanaticism is. The fact that I'd be going home to my family in a funk – a completely avoidable funk that they didn't deserve – pushed me to confront the truths I'd been suppressing.

Real men weren't in the stands that day, their esteem at the mercy of the outcome. They were on the field playing, or coaching. Or somewhere else, achieving *their* goals, doing *their* thing. How had I been so stupid for so long?

Being a fan was a welcome distraction when I was a young buck in the Air Force. Watching the team succeed and feeling like I was somehow a part of it was a fun fantasy when I needed one.

But I was an adult now, living a real life, with real responsibilities. It was past time to put away childish things.

Plus, for all the good times, when things went wrong for the team, they tended to go *really* wrong. And even when they went right, why the hell was *I* celebrating? Why was *I* gloating? What made me ever think wearing the same colors as the men competing entitled me to credit or blame for their success or failure?

Millions are just as consumed and misguided. And there are strong psychological drivers behind the craze that the multi-*billion*-dollar sports industry knows how to exploit.

Oh, you thought we just naturally fell into fanhood? Nope. Sports fan psychology is a serious discipline, and marketers know exactly how to use their findings to make us watch more, care more, *spend* more.

I drug my family through eight more years of fanhood after the Wyoming loss. And that tenth loss to Florida was not fun.

But the embarrassment of the outburst that followed was precisely the shock I needed. Luckily, you don't have to repeat it. For the further I walked from the scene of the meltdown, the clearer the truth became.

Part II

Puberty

Chapter 8
The Talk

We need to have a little talk. The awkward bottom line is this:

Fans are essentially cheerleaders, and cheerleading is not manly.

Competing is. The brawn-on-brawn battle, the athletic excellence, the discipline, the sacrifice, the perseverance. If you're actually *on* the field, *in* the arena, great.

But for the rest of us, playing dress-up in our cute team colors? Rah rah rahing? Gloating when "we" win? Whining and moaning when "we" lose? Prancing around in our hero's jersey?

"#16's *my* favorite! He's the best!"

Screaming when he screws up?

"Throw the ball – *why can't you just throw it?*"

Is this the behavior of real men? Of course not.

Now, I know what you're thinking.

"But I'm *loyal.* Loyalty is manly. Only punks abandon their team. Right?"

Wrong. Punks *switch* teams. Men release the foolishness of team idolatry altogether. Loyalty talk is just a cult retention tactic, another way the sports marketing vampires keep their customers – which is all we are to them – ignorant, subdued and spending.

I suppose if you're going to be a cheerleader, cheering for strangers in the same outfit is better than cheering for whichever strangers happen to be winning. But we are not, nor do we aspire to be, cheerleaders.

"But my team *needs* me."

No, "your" team doesn't know who you are, and they don't care.

Your pretend relationship with Tom Brady or Conor McGregor or LeBron James is sad. Acting as if your cheers have anything to do with their success is pathetic.

Somehow grown men (including me) have been tricked into thinking it's cool and macho to walk around in public in sports stars' jerseys. Where I come from, wearing a player's jersey in high school meant you were dating...

If you really are dating Tony Romo, good for you. But if you're not, reconsider your dignity.

Unlike most fans, I actually had a slight connection to the Vols. I hold four degrees from the University of Tennessee. I wrote most of my dissertation in a graduate student office in the belly of Neyland Stadium (20 yards from where I threatened that poor Florida drummer).

I didn't just go to UT, I taught there. I taught players: Saints Super Bowl-winning wide receiver Robert Meachem. Basketball guard now playing pro in Brazil Cam Tatum. Linebacker turned coach at Albany State Nick Reveiz. (Son of NFL placekicker and local sports commentator Fuad Reveiz, Nick could bench press a horse with one hand and write an A-grade essay with the other.) All of them fine men. All winners in their own right.

Former football coach Phil Fulmer and basketball coach Bruce Pearl visited classes I was teaching to guest speak – Fulmer twice. I shook their hands, took pictures with them, got autographs. Me and Phil even emailed a bit. For a cheerleader, it was quite the thrill.

Fulmer was a gentleman. Pearl, nice enough. But I'm sure both saw me for the fanboy schmuck I was. How could they not? It's hard to respect a man who's gushing all over you. It's hard for a doer to see a cheerer as equal.[3]

---

[3] It should be obvious by now that comparing cheerleaders to fans is actually too generous. Real

If a genuine friend or family member actually coaches or plays for "your" team, go ahead – paint your face, trash up your car, pout after a big loss. (Boy, did I pout after big losses...)

But I'm willing to bet you have no real connection. Maybe you live in the same state or the same city, or maybe you share the same school. But that's a weak basis for the mouth-foaming devotion sports fans are encouraged to show.

Our families, our friends, our (good) neighbors – these are the people who deserve our loyalty. Strangers who play with balls? No.

---

cheerleaders are legit athletes, bear grueling practice schedules, perform under the harshest of conditions, often compete at elite levels, and execute gymnastics moves most men couldn't touch in their prime. Fans, on the other hand, stand and yell at best.

For college sports fans in particular, this doesn't mean we shouldn't be proud of or stop supporting our alma maters (I still am and still do). All it means is that when strangers play a made-up game, regardless of where they play it, it has nothing to do with us. Their performance is theirs. Our performance is ours. The two are not intertwined.

Cheering for a sports team *used* to make you feel edgy. Somehow, as if by magic, the power and success of the team transferred to anyone who rooted for them.

No matter how many thousands of fans pretended along with us, the machismo we once drew from our misplaced idols was never real. Manliness by association is not a thing.

So say it with me: "The more passionate the fan, the more flamboyant the cheerleader." Tacky, but true.

To recap, being a "loyal" fan isn't honorable, it's pathetic. Punks switch teams, cheerleaders stick with "their" team, and real men don't cheer for ball-playing strangers in the first place.

Obvious, yet forbidden truths. Truths that hurt. But admitting them is key.

Chapter 9
Fan Brainwashing 101

If we had to teach a class on how to brainwash sports fans (maybe a class for rookie sports marketers), we wouldn't have any trouble finding source material. Psychologists have been hard at work cracking the sports fan's psyche for decades, and they haven't been shy about sharing their findings with the industry.

As you review the following examples of just how sophisticated and devious sports marketing has become, reflect on how many of these techniques your own team has used to brainwash you.

Exhibit A: "Creating and Fostering Fan Identification in Professional Sports" from *Sports Marketing Quarterly,* Volume VI, Number 1.[4] This foundational gem is chockfull of proven, science-backed techniques for hooking and deepening the emotional investment of sports fans. Take strategy #1, for example: Link the team to the community's traditions, landmarks, and history.

> "The expression of common symbols, history, shared goals, and the fan's need to belong links the team to the community and provides an identity for the team that is inseparable from that of the community. As an embodiment of

---

[4] Yes, Sports Marketing Quarterly is a thing. There were five volumes before this one in 1997, and it's still in print.

the community, a fan's affinity for his or her community is associated and extended to the team."[5]

Of course, teams don't *deserve* this extended affinity. The players are strangers, and in many cases not even from the communities they pretend to represent.

But if the UT marketing department can convince the Vols to charge onto the field carrying the Tennessee state flag, if they can give ESPN footage of the Great Smoky Mountains or Tennessee Walking Horses to run between commercial breaks, if they can convince announcers to call the Vols "Tennessee" rather than "the Vols,"

---

[5] "Creating and Fostering Fan Identification in Professional Sports" by Sutton, McDonald, Milne and Cimperman, Sports Marketing Quarterly. Volume VI, Number 1, 1997, page 19.

well, homesick Airmen will be more likely to believe that the strangers in orange are an extension of the family and culture they love and miss so much.

This propaganda usually goes unnoticed, probably because we want it to be true. If, in a moment of clarity, a Crimson Tide fan wonders why the University of Alabama football team is referred to as "Bama" rather than "the University of Alabama football team," he likely doesn't wonder for long. After all, why not pretend the team's excellence is a reflection of the excellence embodied by his entire state?

In fact, why not pretend the team's excellence is a reflection of *his personal* excellence? This fantasy that a team's achievements are our own is especially dangerous. Which leads us to...

Strategy #2: Encourage fans to confuse the players' performance with their own.

> "Fans look to sport as a means of belonging. Teams should strive to promote this sense of belonging and affiliation. Teams need to communicate the fact that the fans are 'part of the team,' that this is 'their team' and that 'WE' compete together as a unit."[6]

There it is in black and white, explicit direction to blur the line between competitor and spectator. The locker

---

[6] "Creating and Fostering Fan Identification in Professional Sports" by Sutton, McDonald, Milne and Cimperman, Sports Marketing Quarterly. Volume VI, Number 1, 1997, page 21.

room interviews, behind-the-scenes mini-documentaries, overt "we" talk from announcers and promotions – all designed to hitch your identity to their revenue stream.

Does it work? Have you ever caught yourself saying:

> "*We* sure whooped Georgia Saturday!"

or

> "*Our* pitching was wicked killah against the Mets!"

Yeah, me too. When we've indulged in the "we" talk that the industry so enthusiastically encourages, it's evidence of what the sports fan psychologists call "Basking In Reflected Glory" or "BIRGing."

BIRGing not only lets us pretend that our team's awesomeness equates to our personal awesomeness, its tendency to happen in public adds the allure of feeling like we're part of a clan.

Imagine you're in Austin at the 7-Eleven during Oklahoma week. The cashier notices your UT (University of Texas: the *other* UT) hat and gives an approving nod. Then Wednesday Bob from accounting sees your burnt orange tie and throws up a "hook 'em horns" gang sign. Then Sunday you're buying pickles at Walmart and some stranger puts his arm around you, starts talking about how "we" pulled it out in the 4th against those dirty Sooners. Before you know it, you're high fiving, fist-bumping, and inviting him to meet your mom.

Remember: it's a marketing trick. Just because everyone around us pretends "we" talk is legit doesn't make it so. "We" didn't do jack. Win, lose, or draw, "they" competed, not us. Take credit for *your* accomplishments, not the accomplishments of strangers. If you're going to claim a clan, make it one you actually deserve.

Strategy #3: Present flamboyant cheerleading not only as normal, but admirable, enviable, cool.

Have you ever seen an overly absorbed fan and thought, "Damn, *that* guy needs to get a life"? *That* guy's image is suppressed for a reason. (In case you haven't realized it, in someone's eyes at some point, *that* guy was you and me.)

To keep the profits flowing, not only does the industry need to keep us convinced that the team's fate equals our own, but the myth that cheerleading is honorable and manly has to be constantly defended.

> "[M]arketing communications should reinforce and display positive group behaviors of attending an event and following a team, as well as positive attributes of the fan group. Again, fans want to be associated with positive others. If the followers of a team are perceived in a positive way, more fans will be attracted to the fan group and, in turn, the team."[7]

Whether it's an ad for beer or satellite TV, the ideal sports fan is

---
[7] Ibid, page 21.

rugged, successful, and fit enough to jump in and play wide receiver (or at least placekicker) should Coach need him. They'll occasionally mix in a weirdo for comic relief. But what you'll rarely see are the outbursts, the weekends robbed of meaning, the dreams and loved ones neglected in pursuit of the worship of their product.

The ultimate "fanhood is cool" trick happens when athletes are portrayed as fans. Charles Barkley obsesses over his March Madness bracket, Joe Montana frets his fantasy lineup. Athletes are fans, so fans are like athletes, right? Wrong – sports stars are sports stars precisely because they've *not* wasted their lives cheering rather than doing.

The industry encourages the confusion for a simple reason – the more deluded we are, the more money we'll spend and the longer we'll suffer alongside a team that's struggling. In essence, when sports marketers do their jobs, we're more broke and less happy. Three cheers for sports marketers!

Given that most franchises are not perennial champions, how to keep us watching and spending during a slump is of special interest to the industry, leading us straight to...

Exhibit B: A fancy-worded study targeting fans of an unnamed university in the South. If it wasn't so devious, all their big-brained attention might be flattering...

> "The latent moderated structural equations procedure (LMS) was used to examine the moderation effect of identification with the

team. Results indicate that sport consumers' behavioral intentions significantly differed based on game outcome. After a win, consumer emotions were related to both types of satisfaction (i.e., game and service), and game satisfaction mediated the relationship between emotions and behavioral intention. Consumer emotions resulting from a loss, however, did not influence service satisfaction. These findings can help sport organizations understand the emotion-satisfaction-behavior process of sport consumers and design appropriate recovery strategies, such as allocating resources and effort to deliver the highest level of ancillary services to help consumers cope after core service failure."[8]

What I *think* they're saying is that most fans won't abandon ship after "core service failure" (aka a string of losses) so long as they're pacified with "ancillary services," aka the crap the first study recommended: "Your team = your community" and "*WE're* in this together" propaganda.

And they're right. Real fans of bad teams will not only stick by them, they'll wear their suffering as a badge of honor. I've flown team flags on my car after a

---

[8] "The Influence of Emotions on Game and Service Satisfaction and Behavioral Intention in Winning and Losing Situations: Moderating Effect of Identification with the Team" by Yim and Byon, Fit Publishing of West Virginia University.
http://fitpublishing.com/articles/influence-emotions-game-and-service-satisfaction-and-behavioral-intention-winning-and

big loss to thumb my nose at fans of the winning team, but to also show those less committed what a true fan looks like.

If Metallica had to describe this in a song: *"Sad but trooouuwaaahhh!"* If Trump had to do it in a tweet: "Sad!"

Even sadder, some fans seem to actually *prefer* it when their team loses. Losing fuels feelings of superiority over the coaches and gives fans an excuse to piss and moan on social media. "That coach doesn't know what he's doing – fire the bum!" When others agree, it reinforces the solidarity of the cheer tribe, even if it's become a bitter, miserable cheer tribe.

Rather than doubling down or joining in on the bitching, some fans will eventually distance themselves from losses by "Cutting Off Reflective Failure" or "CORFing." The usual "we" talk becomes "they" talk, as in "*They* didn't play worth a damn Sunday."

This is understandable in light of just how hard some fans take big losses (I've been there). But too much CORFing scares the industry. To deter it, they've developed techniques to turn marginal fans into committed supporters, and committed supporters into rabid fanatics.

In fact, there's a "Fan Involvement Ladder" developed by psychology professor Daniel Wann at Murray State University in Kentucky. The progression: Suspect → Prospect → Customer → Client → Member → Advocate → Raving Fan. For strategies on how to move fans up the ladder, look no further than...

Exhibit C: A study by researchers from the Universities of Oregon and Louisville on how to turn passive fans into big spenders and big spenders into contributors for life.[9]

For the bubbliest of cheerleaders (this is probably you, so pay attention), the idea is to never allow them to doubt their fanhood, and to milk them for all they're worth.

> "Because they are so valuable to the team, marketers want to avoid a situation in which highly loyal fans would decrease their behavior or reconsider their allegiance to their favorite team... The objective

---

[9] "Using the Psychological Commitment to Team (PCT) Scale to Segment Sport Consumers Based on Loyalty" by Mahonny and Madrigal, Sport Marketing Quarterly. Vol 1, No 1, 2000.
https://business.uoregon.edu/files/media/madrigal-using-psychological-commitment_1.pdf

is to progressively increase the yield from these best consumers..."[10]

That's right – block fanhood to manhood transformations in order to "progressively increase yield." *That's* how you're truly thought of and treated. You're not a member or a contributor; you're worth nothing more than your purchasing power, and treated pretty much the same way dairy farmers treat cows.

For fans who attend games but aren't emotionally dependent enough, the experts recommend highlighting the team's tradition or its first-rate treatment of patrons. And if all else fails, feign support for a social cause.

---
[10] Ibid, page 23.

"A team, for example, that demonstrates its commitment to helping battered women by pledging a portion of each ticket sold to fund or construct a new shelter provides the spuriously loyal fan one more important reason to care about the organization and to attend games."

For frugal fans, make purchases easier with entry-level products like mini season ticket packages. And for the dreaded low-loyalty fan, try luring them in "by offering packages to various groups (e.g., families, businesses)."[11]

By attracting families, teams not only entice thrifty dads to open their wallets, but they lay the foundation for

---

[11] Ibid, page 24.

little Timmy's adulthood addiction. How? Enmeshing a boy's memories of a team with memories of family will make questioning fanhood later in life tantamount to questioning Grandpa. One commentator from Penn State put it like this:

> "Interestingly, there is an overwhelmingly structured 'path' to becoming a sports fanatic. The introduction usually occurs around the age of 8 or 9, when children become very susceptible to long-term emotional attachment... Understandably, the strongest influences of sports team attachment come from the immediate family or friends... Thinking about this makes it clear that the sports industry tries to

capture children very early by attracting families and investing in peoples' loyal fandom."[12]

Funny, my first fanhood memory: watching the Vols take on the Hurricanes in the '86 Sugar Bowl with my parents and sister, looking for my Aunt Dot in the crowd on TV. I was eight. Next: the '87 UT-California matchup at Neyland Stadium with my dad at age ten. No wonder by the time I left for the Air Force the Vols felt like family.

No wonder that 20 years later I was a co-conspirator in my own kids' brainwashing. On top of dressing them in cutesy team garb, plastering team stickers on their crib and taking them to

---

[12] "Our Irrational Passion for Sports" by Suresh Rajan. http://sites.psu.edu/academy/2014/09/29/irrational-passion/

games, I enrolled them in UT's "Jr. Vols Kids Club." Membership included free tickets to everything but football games, team-themed art projects (I remember my oldest filling a plastic football statuette with orange and white sand), and team mascot coloring books. As the website pitches today, "Join the fun and connect with your favorite team in a fun and engaging way!"[13]

This isn't isolated or unique. When I took my kids to a Nationals game in DC, they were awarded a free pack of baseball cards and a "first game" certificate to hang in their bedroom. Nashville's Titans have a Kids Club ("More Events! More Fun!"), as do most NFL teams.[14] The Bulls have a "Chicago

---

[13] https://utsports.com/sports/2017/6/14/fans-jr-vols-html.aspx

[14] https://www.titansonline.com/fans/kids-club

Bulls Kid Nation" affiliated with the NBA's Jr. NBA program.[15] Your (old) team probably does something similar.

To their credit, some programs include youth camps where kids get the chance to actually *play* sports rather than watch. But the ultimate financial motivation is clear. Public relations and social media strategist Victoria Shelton explained it well while studying at Samford.

> "While the short-term goal of these programs is to boost attendance and increase revenue sales, the long-term goal is to help create lifelong fans who will support the team for years to come. By offering special promotions and giveaways to entice fans when

---

[15] https://www.nba.com/bulls/kidnation

they are young, sports marketers are instilling a love of the team in these kids that will only grow as they continue to grow."[16]

And Kenneth Cortsen, a sports business researcher, put it like this:

"Simply, the above-mentioned examples provide perfect ways to build emotional equity with the youngest fan groups and thus with the long-term fans of the club. This is a great way to secure future revenue streams."[17]

---

[16] "Developing Diehards: The Power of Marketing Sports to Children." https://www.samford.edu/sports-analytics/fans/2017/Developing-Diehards-The-Power-of-Marketing-Sports-to-Children

[17] Cortsen of course wasn't referring to the examples I've provided, but others you can read about yourself in "Football Marketing Targeting Kids" at http://kennethcortsen.com/football-marketing-targeting-kids/

Philip Morris understood that a customer at ten is a customer for life. It looks like the sports industry has taken a few lessons from Big Tobacco.

Reflect on your own fanhood memories. Your childhood keep popping up? Family? That's no accident.

Exhibit D: A 2013 paper co-written by researchers in Minnesota and Portugal on "Spectator-Based Brand Equity."

> "Results gathered from a confirmatory factor analysis indicated an acceptable fit of the model to the data and confirmed the relationship between Internalization, a single first-order construct, and Brand Associations, a second-order construct with ten dimensions. Review of the

psychometric properties indicated all constructs had good internal consistency, convergent validity, and discriminant validity."[18]

Second-order constructs with ten dimensions? Psychometric properties and discriminant validity?

Guys, when I say the industry isn't fooling around, they're *really* not fooling around. The literature is rife with jargon-filled research just like this, furthering marketers' understanding of how to reel us in and keep us hooked. They've clocked hundreds of thousands of hours figuring out how to make us care and spend more, with little concern for

---

[18] "Spectator-Based Brand Equity in Professional Soccer" by Biscaia, Correia, Ross, Rosado and Maroco, Sports Marketing Quarterly, March, 2013.
https://sportmarketingassociation.wordpress.com/2013/03/18/spectator-based-brand-equity-in-professional-soccer/

whether it's good for us, our families or our communities.

Chariot race fanatics in ancient Rome had only themselves to blame. But today nobody passively slips into fanhood. We're targeted, kidnapped and waterboarded with "Go team!" Kool-Aid until we eventually succumb.

Maybe it's not *that* dramatic. But sports fan psychology really is a thing, and your team's marketing department really has been using it against you, likely from a young age.

Let the fact that you have an old and active enemy inspire perseverance as you begin the next crucial step: *the purge.*

Chapter 10
The Purge

I need you to get your team garbage away from your person and out of your sight ASAP.

Disentangling the team's identity from your identity begins with changing the clothes on your back, the stickers on your car, even the background on your phone.

If you're like I was, burning it on the spot isn't an option – too much emotion (and money – that crap was expensive) invested to just trash it.

So baby steps are fine. But we need all those reminders of your past addiction away from you *now*.

This can be tough. The memories and the (fabricated) sense of belonging make the sports fan's addiction intimate. But if I could do it, you can do it.

After the drummer boy incident, I put all of my Vols crap in a box and relegated it to the garage. The shirts, the hats, even the paraphernalia: the limited-edition tailgate party cast iron '39 Ford complete with Smokey dog mascot, cooler, and grille, the Neyland Stadium replica, the game day cup with dozens of tickets from all the games I'd wasted my time and money on, complete with the '98 Florida game victory (a victory that had absolutely nothing to do with me) end zone grass at the bottom.

All of it, in a box, straight to the garage.

I didn't actually get rid of anything until months later. Most of it I eventually gave to nephews, though I should have sent it to the dump – you don't see recovering crackheads donating their old pipes to family members. But whatever you choose to do with your team trinkets, we need them out of sight, out of mind, now.

Further, I hereby declare your gaudy, overpriced officially licensed team clothing part of a cheerleading uniform, and wearing it the same as wearing a pink cheerleading skirt.[19]

---

[19] Hopefully the emphasis on cheerleaders and skirts is resonating. But if it's not, hang with me. I needed to make fanhood as unattractive as possible to self-cure, and this was a big part of it. But as you'll soon find, there's much more to the process. Just as the military molds new recruits, first we tear down, then we build up.

Pretending along with the rest of a society that a cartwheel just ain't a cartwheel unless everyone can see your bloomers, short skirts are the quintessential element of cheerleading attire. Intentionally effeminate and flirtatious, my wife was a cheerleader, and I love to see her in a skirt.

However, I do not aspire to be a cheerleader, and neither do you. Shaking pom-poms is the opposite of the fanhood fantasy, but much closer to the truth. So to make it as real and repulsive as possible, team gear = pink skirt.

Your $100 Red Wings jersey, beat-up Duke cap with the hologram sticker, Seahawks sweatshirt your cousin gave you for Christmas – regardless of the costs or connections, putting on anything and everything team-branded immediately causes a pink cheerleading skirt to appear around your waist. Neither the success of the franchise, nor the price of the item, nor the story behind it diminishes this fact. Team gear = pink skirt.

Just as Fat Albert couldn't keep wearing his "I'm Hard to Kidnap" t-shirt and expect to grow a six pack, you can't keep wearing your old team gear and expect to beat fanhood. You have to change your outward appearance before you can change your inner self.

So in a box. To the garage (or back of a closet). Now.

Chapter 11
Taking Stock

The same weekend of my purge I decided I needed to further distance myself from the program. No disrespect to the players and coaches who'd been putting in the work, doing the manly competing thing. But as a fan, thanks to Urban Meyer, Tim Tebow, bad calls and tough breaks, one game – the Florida game – had hurt worse than the rest.

This made '05-'14 an especially rough decade. Each annual loss came with the dread that "we" wouldn't get another chance to beat them for 364 days. Another year of having to put up with local Gator fans' gloating (gloating that was not only childish and sissified, but completely unearned for them as well), another year of wondering, in vain, when the horrid streak would end.

As the years added up, the embarrassment took its toll. You start to develop an inferiority complex. A *completely undeserved* inferiority complex, but an inferiority complex nonetheless.

There had been a time in my life when being a fan was a decent gamble. Being an Airman in the desert often sucked, and living through Peyton Manning (as pathetic as this was) made the suckage tolerable.

But I had grown up, started a family, accomplished a few things. Did fanhood as a source of esteem still make sense?

The more I thought about it, the more I realized I'd been quietly kicking butt. So I typed up a comparison to make the distinction clearer.

Year	Vols	Me
2005	Lost to Gators	Graduated College Summa Cum Laude
2006	Lost to Gators	Taught my First College Class
2007	Lost to Gators	Earned a Master's Degree
2008	Lost to Gators	Became a Dad
2009	Lost to Gators	Founded an Ethics Bowl
2010	Lost to Gators	Became a Part-Time Comedy Club Host
2011	Lost to Gators	Fathered a Daughter; Celebrated Ten Years of Marriage; Earned a Ph.D.
2012	Lost to Gators	Became a Presidential Management Fellow; Worked for the Congressional Research Service on Capitol Hill

| 2013 | Lost to Gators | Finished my First Book |
| 2014 | Lost to Gators | Acquired Land for my Family's "Forever Home"[20] |

Approaching 40, I wasn't a rock star. But I wasn't a homesick kid anymore, either. Continuing to tie my happiness to a sports team was especially foolish in light of all I'd done and was doing.

But even if I hadn't been kicking butt, even if *you* haven't been kicking butt (make a list and see), all the time and energy I'd spent obsessing over a team could have been spent planning and living *my* life, building memories of *my* big plays.

---

[20] I prefer to call it our "terminal residence," but my wife does not.

You'd think I would have figured this out before 37. But that Sugar Bowl win when I was a boy, the reinforcement during my time in the Air Force, and especially the national championship when I came home in '98, had me sucked in deep. The marketing ploys probably hadn't hurt.

The scary thing is had that losing streak not reached the magic number of ten, *I'd almost certainly still be asleep.* Even worse, I might have indoctrinated my kids beyond rescue, gifting the industry three long-term revenue streams.

If your (former) team's blessed you with a losing streak, be glad! Not all fans are so lucky.

If they're currently winning, escape will be tougher. But you can do it, and understanding the true purpose of spectator sports will make the breakup easier.

Chapter 12
All About the Benjamins

Whether it's the NCAA, NFL, NBA, MLB, NHL, NASCAR, UFC, MLS or any of the hundreds of soccer/football leagues around the world (damn, those soccer fans get crazy), PGA (are there rabid golf fans?) or any other hyper-monetized spectator sport, fans are revenue sources, plain and simple. We are customers and the entertainment (as well as the sad sense of belonging) teams provide is the product.

You saw in our sports psych research exposé how we are to be wooed up the Psychological Commitment to Team scale, the craziest among us carefully courted in order to "progressively increase yield" (bonus fan bucks milked from our team-colored teets), our children treated as long-term investments, groomed for harvest. Mr. Burns ain't got nothin' on sports marketers.

Additional clues that it's all about the Benjamins:

- Officially licensed Christmas ornaments, bottle openers, and bras. As one Auburn exec said to another, "Will 'War Eagle' fit on it? Trademark that sucker and triple the price!"
- Ticketing schemes that require a "donation" before you can buy. Doesn't the mob do this?
- $7 hotdogs and $5 Cokes. From what I recall from the (now

demolished) Georgia Dome and Nationals Park in DC, price gouging on beer is even worse. Oh, and parking – ridiculously expensive parking.

- Smoke and mirrors slow-motion promo footage, similar to ads you'd see for tactical flashlights or BMWs or any other material thing for sale. Dave Chapelle once did a skit on how slow motion makes everything look cooler, including laundry. That militaristic music overlaying slow-mo tackle breaks and headers for the win? It's a marketing ploy. Stop falling for it.

We could add annual branding catchphrases: "Team 121" or "It's Time" or "Ray Lewis is Innocent, We Swear!"

Or announcers introducing "your" Seattle Seahawks, "your" Pittsburgh Penguins, or "your" whatever. Unless you're Jerry Jones at a Cowboys game, sit down – it's a trick. Exception: Packers shareholders, this one minor point doesn't apply to you... I suppose they technically are "your" Packers. But everyone else, sit down.

Or the fact that college athletes *still* aren't fairly compensated for their sweat, commitment and sacrifice. Maybe one day they'll learn to collectively bargain.

Then there are the product endorsements. Legend has it that Shaq snubbed Wheaties and signed a deal with Fruity Pebbles because he only pitches products he actually uses.[21] Whether

---

[21] Thanks to buddy Matt White for sharing the legend,

Shaq makes a point to cruise the beach in a well-insured red convertible with a cartoon general reeking of Icy Hot, I leave for you to decide. But see if you can keep from imagining that general giving Shaq an Icy Hot massage now that I've introduced the idea.

> "Ooooh, that's the spot, General. Right there..." in that sexy Shaq voice.

Before the scandals broke out, we'd regularly see Tiger Woods professing his love for Buicks. *Buicks?*

> "Play like Tiger? Not a chance. Drive like Tiger? No problem!"

Yeah, no problem if you can afford a C-Class Mercedes. No way Tiger Woods

---

and to Cosmo Frank at Esquire for confirming it in his 2015 interview, "Shaq: 'Did I Retire Too Early? Yes.'"

is jaunting to his mistresses' houses in a mid-range GM. [2021 update: I was sad to see Tiger involved in a Los Angeles car crash in February, and wish him a fast and full recovery. But I must admit scouring news reports for the vehicle make and model, which turned out not to be a Buick.]

Concussions, doping, recruiting scandals – commissioners, owners, and athletic directors look the other way so long as the money keeps flowing. "Deflect and distract" seems the strategy of choice.

To be clear, I'm not saying there's anything wrong with running a business. Businesses are great. Yay, capitalism. Just don't suffer the illusion that professional sports (and in most ways, collegiate sports) are anything more.

But maybe you're okay with this.

"So what? My team's a business. Apple's a business and I *love* Apple."

I enjoy shiny new things, too. But life's too short to spend it chasing the latest Xbox or Yeti cooler. My kids will eventually insist we upgrade, but for now the old school Nintendo Wii is plenty fun enough. And $300 for a cooler? Unless you're transporting human hearts, the $30 Coleman will do.

Confession: I have a thing for old Cadillac Coupe Devilles. My first car was a green '75, I drove an '84 in the Air Force (on which I flew those silly orange flags), and I own a white '77 now (a college graduation gift from Dad). A convertible 60s model is in the ten-year plan.

But I don't *worship* Cadillac. I don't plan my schedule around their product releases or base my self-esteem on how highly the brand is ranked by J.D. Power. It's a company, and their execs couldn't care less about me. Plus, Cadillac stopped making Devilles over a decade ago, so screw those guys.

It's the same with sports. Down at the fan's level, it's easy to forget that it's neither glory, nor pride, nor love of the game truly driving the spectacle. It's the almighty dollar.

> "But what about Mark Cuban? Being a Dallas Mavericks fan is different. Our owner's a fan just like us – we're one big family!"

Mark Cuban may dress and behave like a typical (non-billionaire) Mavs fan. But he's not some random rich dude in a t-shirt and jeans. Cuban hires the coach. He negotiates the players' salaries. He buys the training equipment, recruits the team doctor, approves the shoes.

Mr. Cuban's among the few people who actually *deserve* to get excited when the Mavs win. Plus, the more excited he looks, the more validated his customers feel. Validated customers = more merchandise and ticket sales = more *cha-ching.*

If Mr. Cuban happens to care about his players, good for him. If he wants the honorable citizens of Dallas to be happy, great. But he's businessman (and a darn good one from what I've seen on Shark Tank).

There's nothing wrong with an owner getting excited about those extra millions flowing into their bank account, especially when their team's success really is a reflection of their personal efforts, and especially when showing that excitement will boost profits even more. Just don't use an owner's legitimate passion to rationalize mere customers'.

Chapter 13
Bring It On!

So team gear is the same as a cheerleading uniform, team trinkets are akin to crack pipes, and above the players, above the coaches, above the managers lie greedy execs and athletic directors in smoke-filled rooms plotting next season's merchandising push. At their side are sports fan psychologists revealing the latest research on how to seduce little Johnny and convince you to put this book down and turn on the game.

Painful truths, I know. But you're getting used to them, so let's crank reality up another notch.

Ever see *Bring It On?* From what I've caught flipping through the channels, it's about snotty cheerleaders insulting one another. Arrogant, petty, looking for a catfight where one needn't be.

Where had I seen this behavior before... Oh yeah, in the mirror!

The next time you see a man strutting around in team gear, imagine those sassy cheerleaders – taunting and flaunting. The difference is that the *Bring It On* cheerleaders competed in a dance off, whereas fans don't actually *do* anything.

"Hey, repping my team is like being in a gang!"

Yes, a slothful, whiny, sensitive gang that prances around and gloats. A gang that gets extra gloaty after a big play, flashing their best "*na-nana-boo-boo*" taunts at opposing fans.

> "See how awesome *my* players are? Take that!"

There's this post-win chant I'm ashamed to admit I've sung many times, usually directed at an outnumbered group of the other team's fans:

> "It's great, to be, a Tennessee Vol; I said it's great, to be, a Tennessee Vol; that's right it's great, to be, a Tennessee Vol…"

A catchy tune – maybe you've sung something similar?

Come on. How have we been fooled into thinking this is acceptable or that fans have anything to brag about in the first place?

The men who struggled and triumphed had every reason in the world to be proud – *even when they lost.* Hopefully when they won they could do it with class. But in any case, their fans simply happened to be wearing the same colored outfits. This is supposed to magically transfer their victory onto us how?

But it's a clan thing, you say. "We fans are a tough bunch. If you mess with one of us, you mess with all of us!"

Whatever.

I once saw a drunk Alabama fan outside Neyland yelling at Vol fans after a Tide loss. It was on the backside of the stadium, along a road that loops left towards the Sunsphere (where Knoxville stores its wigs, according to The Simpsons).

Nobody did a thing. Old Alabama boy was cursing and calling one particular Vol fan a fatass, doing his best to get him to fight. Uninterested, his target just wanted to go home. But the drunk guy wouldn't let it go.

None of the hundreds of fellow Vol fans walking by stepped in to defend this guy's victim, including me. So much for the "We're a gang – nobody messes with us!" myth. Nothing more than a bluff.[22]

Maybe, *just maybe,* that was that Bama fan's drummer boy incident. Maybe on the long ride back to Tuscaloosa he reflected on how ridiculous he had been, how he and the man he was accosting could have been friends, and how his life could mean so

---

[22] European soccer hooligans: you're excused from this particular critique. But not the others.

much more than worship of a sports franchise. But I doubt it.

If he stuck with the team just a little longer, he's enjoyed all of those SEC and national championships, probably feeling like I did in '98 when UT won it all after years of frustration. Nick Saban has taken Bama on one heck of a ride (except for that last-second missed field goal return loss to Auburn – ouch). It would be hard *not* to get sucked in given the team's extraordinary success.

But surely a guy upset enough to pick fights with strangers had dreams he was sidelining. I know I sure did.

If you're Saban or one of his five-star studs, then more power to you. But grown men who have nothing to do with the program? Wake up. We're better than that.

I was recently waiting out a layover at the Houston airport and overheard one pinstriped cheerleader yell to another, "*Let's go Yan-kees* (clap clap, clap-clap-clap)." How sweet. A prissy braggart reunion! And within earshot of Astros fans. Not to mention Sox fans who might have been traveling through.

I remember those days, flaunting my colors so fearlessly. I had this orange t-shirt with two words on the front, two on the back.

Front: "Hey Spurrier"

Back: "*Up Yours*"

Steve Spurrier, nationally known simply as the "Head Ball Coach," was UF's football coach at the time –

notoriously antagonistic, and notoriously good.

I wore that classless shirt to Florida games even after Spurrier retired, and then to South Carolina games when he *un*retired to coach the Gamecocks. I also wore it to Pensacola Beach at the height of his run with the Gators.

Such a brave cheerleader, donning my most scandalous skirt so deep behind enemy lines!

The puffed-up boastfulness, the spite, the artificial division. Not cool or manly, but far too common.

I recently passed a Clemson fan on the Laurel Falls trail in the Smoky Mountains. Clemson was awful a decade ago, but they're actually good now (good enough to humble the mighty Alabama program). So this guy would have had something to be proud of... were he a coach or a player.

You could see the tension between him and fans repping other teams – some from Georgia, some from Alabama, probably one from Notre Dame (I actually don't remember seeing an Irish fan, but given their ubiquity, it's a safe bet). For some reason cheerleaders from all over just have to wear their favorite skirt anytime they venture into Tennessee for a hike.

Boys, let's just chill and enjoy the outdoors, alright? The gang/brotherhood thing is made up and stupid and fake. If you need a safe outlet to rebel, I feel you. But let's find a better way.

Whatever your old skirt colors, there are reasons why you allowed the sports media industrial complex to sink its fangs into your soul. Our culture says it's normal, honorable – even patriotic. But nobody gets *that* wrapped up in fanhood unless there are additional drivers at play.

My guess is that it's something you're suppressing, something you're avoiding, something you know you need to be doing but have been using fanhood to avoid.

A little insight into what that thing is will help you overcome the madness. I therefore summon the ghost of Sigmund "Freaknasty" Freud.

Chapter 14
Freud Said *What?*

Freud, the guy who said you have the hots for your mom, taught us that our subconscious minds drive our conscious behavior. And usually, according to Freud, our subconscious minds are thinking about sex.

That 60s model convertible Caddy I want? Something to do with sex. Your job? Sex. That smartphone upgrade you're itching to pull the trigger on? That's sex, too. Freud was a horndog.

If you're skirt-deep in fanhood, there's a reason for it. Maybe it's sex. But most modern psychologists have rejected Freud's overemphasis on the pleasures of the flesh, arguing human psyches are more complex (though only slightly... *mmm, sex...*).

Are you using sports fanaticism as an excuse to drink? To eat garbage? A way to avoid a suppressed dream? (This was part of my problem, as you'll soon find out.)

If your team wins a championship, will that prove to Missy that she shouldn't have rejected you in the 3rd grade when she found out you picked your nose and wiped it on the back of the school bus seat? (Sorry I ratted you out, Eli, but Missy deserved better. You're cool now. But little boy you was gross.)

It could be as simple as getting caught up in the mania. You overhear commuters on the "L" hyping the new shortstop, see "Cubs Win!" on the front page of the Tribune, and suddenly you're checking StubHub for tickets to Saturday's doubleheader at Wrigley. If the marketers have successfully planted the subconscious seed that game time = family time, you invite your nephew, splurge on jerseys, and voila, two new revenue streams.

There's also the thrill of rooting for a team that might very well lose. Then, if it comes, the elation of the collective payoff – at the expense of the fans on the other side (who just as easily could have been the victors).

Sports addicts share much with degenerate gamblers. The same neural pathways that light up when you hit $500 on the slots are probably tickled when your team scores a big win, with underdog victories feeling especially euphoric. Researcher Eric Simons explains this heightened joy in terms of pattern disruption:

> "Since no win is 100 percent certain, every win comes with at least a small [synaptic] reward. But beating your heavily favored rival on the road? That, to your reward center, is hot stuff."[23]

I chased that "hot stuff" feeling three decades straight. And like all addicts, I built up a tolerance. Early in fanhood, a winning record, a franchise player to follow or an occasional victory over a ranked opponent were all it took to keep a smile on my face and my team flags flying. But as the years went on, the bar was raised.

---

[23]*The Secret Lives of Sports Fans*, 2013, page 175.

The Battle of New Orleans planted the seed that our Vols could hang with (and beat!) the best in the country, regardless of what the "experts" predicted (us against the world, baby – who cares what the analysts think). The Manning era taught us that we belonged in the national spotlight, to play in the best bowls, and that beating recurring opponents South Carolina, Kentucky and Vanderbilt was a given.

Pretty soon, games didn't matter – *wins* didn't even matter – unless they were against a highly-ranked opponent, preferably a highly-ranked rival, and preferably in dramatic, underdog comeback fashion. My brain's pleasure center wanted a dopamine flood like it got in '98 when they beat the Gators, or later that year when they won the national championship against Florida State.

But dramatic, underdog comeback wins against highly-ranked rivals are rare. And so I learned firsthand how the seasoned sports fanatic develops a hardened desensitization.

Maybe I'd have been better off at the casino. When you drop a hundred bucks at the blackjack table, at least the dealer doesn't follow you home and rub it in. But when you've publicly committed to a team (with your wardrobe, your social media posts, the bets you've made at work) and they lose, you find belittlement anywhere fans of the winning team lurk. Church is awkward enough without smack talk from Cowboys fan Carl.

"How 'bout them Cowboys?!"

"Yes, Carl. Peace be with you. Now go away."

Don't get the wrong idea. While gambling with money is in many ways less risky than gambling with your identity, we'll talk about healthy replacements for fanhood in the next section. Poker, unsurprisingly, is not on the list.

A lot of Freud's ideas were crazy. Girls do not have "penis envy" (Freud, you freaking weirdo). But his basic argument that "insight" into the motives of our subconscious empowers us to address and modify them still rings true.

When you can *see* what's really happening in your head, you can better change and deal with it. Figuring that out isn't always easy. But try.

Are there triggers that have seemed to make you more or less fanatical? Financial woes, familial expectations, nonsense at work? What drove you to fanaticism in the first place? A tough time away from home like me? Some trauma that distracting yourself with the team helped you overcome?

Whatever the reasons, the more clearly you can bring them into your conscious mind, the more effectively you can address and transcend them. So take some time to reflect – it's worth the trouble.

Hint: It probably has something to do with your mom, you freak.

Part III

Manhood

Chapter 15
What, Then?

"So I'm beginning to understand why I was such a nut. And I'm definitely ready to move on. But so much of my life has revolved around my team. If I didn't have the preseason, the rivalry games, the playoffs to look forward to – what would I do?"

Learn the backstroke. Play the guitar. Build a treehouse. Become a chef. Give your significant other a massage (or Shaq, with Icy Hot). Start a business. Run a 5k. Take your kids on a hike. Volunteer as a Scout leader. Write. Sing.

Learn to throw a football your fucking self. If you're too old to play, become a volunteer coach.

All that sports crap you've been glorifying? Give it a shot! We get one life. One. Don't spend it watching other people live. Vicarious is an awesome song (the band's *Tool* – YouTube it), but a sad way to live.

Think about the cool adventures and goals you've always wanted to pursue, but have neglected in exchange for the safety of cheering. Replacing team fanaticism with an authentic passion will not only make your life more satisfying and enjoyable, it will make your recovery faster, more complete, and permanent.

Addiction therapists know all about the power of replacing negative objects of desire with positive ones.[24] Chewing gum – *lots* of gum – helped me quit smoking. Pursuing the crazy adventure you'll read about in the next chapter not only fulfilled a longtime dream, it helped me quit fanhood.

So don't just stop being a fan. Start being a man. This at the very least means finding meaning, purpose, and satisfaction in *your* pursuits, not the pursuits of strangers who play with balls.

The "what" and "how" are up to you. Some fans have been suppressing business goals. Others athletic goals (maybe I'll see you on American Ninja Warrior a year from now?). Others spiritual goals. It all depends on what seems right for you.

---

[24] Credit old pal and phenomenal musician Doug Sneed for offering this insight.

But you'll know you've found a worthwhile alternative to fanhood – a positive outlet for that misplaced time and attention – when it meets three criteria:

a) It's a little **s**cary
b) It feels **a**uthentic
c) You envision yourself being **p**roud on the other side

Scary, **A**uthentic, and **P**roud. Crap. Looks like our acronym is **SAP**.

Maybe this advice is a little sappy. But I'm okay with that. We can pretend we're too cool to care about what we do or don't accomplish in this short life, and that our culture's "manquilizer" is legit.

It's your choice. You can take the blue pill, gather 'round the tube to belch, squeal, and indulge in the old crew's slavish passivity.

Or you can take the red pill and continue down the rabbit hole, only now at a sprint.

I chose the latter. And had the time of my life.

Chapter 16
Midlife Crisis MMA

Remember Ralphie's bully from *A Christmas Story?* I unfortunately had my own Scut Farkus. My Scut didn't have freckles or wear a coonskin cap. But he did have squinty eyes and a similar gift for harassing kids younger and smaller.

My Scut happened to ride my school bus. He'd sit behind me and flip my ear, or beside me and frog my arm, always just out of sight of the bus driver. Sometimes he'd mix things up and frog my leg instead, always remembering to remind me how much of a pussy I was.

A year older and always bigger, he started around kindergarten and continued into high school. Why I never snapped and busted his nose (or shoved a drumstick up his ass), I don't know. I guess I got conditioned to take it. Though I really wanted to, I never mustered the courage to fight back. And my failure to stand up for myself, despite hundreds of opportunities, was an enduring shame.

Though I'd grown up, served in the military, earned a fancy degree and started a family, I'd never fully shaken it. Boyhood me had been a habitual coward, and adult me couldn't fully forgive myself.

You saw in the Taking Stock chapter that this hadn't stopped me from accomplishing a few things. But my embarrassing past was always there, unfinished business for which I had yet to atone.

I often fantasized redemption. No, not tracking Scut down and putting his eye out with a Red Ryder BB gun. That was years ago. You can't judge a man for what he did as a boy. I'm not the same person. Neither is he.

Rather, my redemption fantasy involved boxing or kickboxing, or even doing a mixed martial arts fight. Competitively fighting – something *waaaaay* outside my comfort zone – would prove I wasn't a wimp anymore.

But fighting was for other guys, tougher guys – *waaaaay* tougher than me. Plus my prime (if I'd ever had one) had long since passed. That dream would just have to remain a dream.

But on the day of the drummer boy incident I was 37 – *just* old enough for an early midlife crisis. Walking from the scene of the meltdown, searching my soul as to why I had gotten so upset, in addition to seeing the terrible example I was setting for my kids, I realized it wasn't too late to pursue my dream. Considering a possible world in which I never did it, I imagined myself at 85 in a rocking chair, reflecting:

> "You always wanted to fight, but never had the guts. *Pussy.* You had one life. Now it's too late."

The thought of living out my days without fight footage to watch with my grandkids or old stinky wrist wraps to chase them around with was terrifying. Despite anything else I'd done or would do, the shame of never getting in the ring would be unbearable.

So I mentally committed to take the plunge. I joined a boxing gym, started working with an MMA team, and set an unforgettable midlife crisis adventure in motion.

I had no illusions of becoming a UFC champion. I just needed one fight to prove to my 37 and 85-year-old selves that I could do it. I needed to become the hero that boyhood me deserved.

The journey wasn't easy. Black eyes, a busted (possibly cracked) nose, exhausted (and possibly concussed) so badly that I had to pull over on the way home after a kickboxing fight and throw up.

But was it worth it?

You're damn right it was worth it. Here's what I wrote in my journal after my first boxing match:

It was an awesome experience: being one of the fighters amongst the audience beforehand, getting my hands taped and "gloved up," stepping through the ropes and under the lights, sitting on a stool and spitting in a bucket during the breaks (just like in the movies), slugging it out for three solid rounds and shaking lots of supportive fans' hands afterwards.

I won't spoil the story, but my second boxing fight went even better than my first. Then it was time to transition to kickboxing.

During the 3rd round of my first match I had what I've come to call my "Bloodsport Moment." I was getting tired, and my opponent – a tattooed, shaved-headed dude 14 years my junior named *Logan Steele* (has there ever been a scarier kickboxer name?) – landed a series of hard headshots that left me woozy.

The worst of them was a "Superman" punch. Logan, who it turns out had far more fighting experience than his coach disclosed to the promoters, reared back as if he was going to throw a roundhouse kick to my thigh, but instead lunged forward like the Man of Steel flying into Zod, bringing all his weight to bear through his knuckles, into my jaw.

I was rocked like never before. In a daze, a voice came to me:

> "Oh man, I'm about to get knocked out. Maybe I should just let him. If

I get knocked out, I can finally rest... And I've never had that experience before. Maybe it's a cool buzz?"

Allowing myself to get knocked out made a surprising amount of sense. Rest is good. I was tired. Why not?

But as that voice had me almost convinced, another voice, a louder voice from deeper inside, replied:

"No! *Hit that son of a bitch!* Keep pushing – no stopping!"

The momentum had been in his favor. I was hurt, exhausted, and thanks to some weak voice from the ether, considering giving up, expecting him to knock me unconscious any moment.

My weaker side was ready to accept that fate. "Rest. Enjoy the buzz!"

But my stronger side knew getting knocked unconscious would *not* be a cool experience. I'd worked for this for months. I only had to go another round, and I knew I could do it.

Despite being near what I thought was my physical breaking point, despite having had the shit kicked out of me, I kept going, kept pushing, kept hitting. I persevered and he backed down.

Watching Peyton Manning throw touchdowns on TV never made me so tired I threw up. I never got a black eye shaking a pom-pom. But I wouldn't trade that and dozens of other memories, or the proof in my home office – a "fight of the night" trophy, a winner's medal, the pictures – for anything.

Boyhood wuss me: vindicated. Midlife crisis challenge: complete. Fanhood: shed.

I learned a lot about my approach to obstacles (straightforward, persistent), how much my family means to me, and that I'm far tougher than I ever knew.

You can read the intimate details in *Year of the Fighter: Lessons from my Midlife Crisis Adventure*. It includes my life-changing and affirming story, what I learned about launching and completing cool adventures (some of which you're getting here), what it felt like to fight (sometimes beat, sometimes get beaten by) guys half my age, meet my coach – a Golden Gloves champ who went three rounds with Floyd "Money" Mayweather back in the day – as well as a former meth dealer (the dude who called me a "moving punching bag") saved by boxing and Jesus, the local Chuck Norris (whose car wash I kinda stole from when I was a teenager...), and even learn my real name (my day job was/is too tame to publish this openly).

Shedding fanhood and embracing my manhood (ripping off a skirt and grabbing my crotch? No) was one of the best decisions of my life. The big, crazy, awesome thing that I'd always wanted to do, but had never mustered the guts to do – the thing I was running from, which had pushed me into the depths of fanhood – *I did it.*

But we're not here to relive my post-fanhood triumph. We're here to kickstart yours.

Chapter 17
The Formula

Deep down, you've known for a while that fanhood is a waste. Everybody does. We're just too scared (or too polite – this truth hurts) to say it out loud.

You're also gaining a little insight into the reasons that have driven and kept you there. An excuse? A distraction? An avoidance?

You've also reviewed my criteria for selecting life-affirming adventures that will supplant your former fixation on a team: they're a little **s**cary, they feel **a**uthentic (consistent with the real you), and you envision being **p**roud on the other side. The corny acronym that sticks: **SAP.**

Have something in mind? Good. You're now ready for the three steps that will make your 85-year-old self (and your current self) smile. I cover these in more depth in *Year of the Fighter.* But in a nutshell, they are:

1. **C**ommit
2. **B**egin
3. **R**esearch

CBR happens to be the name of Honda's sportiest crotch rocket. So to remember **C**ommit, **B**egin, **R**esearch, just picture yourself popping a wheelie on a tricked-out sport bike.

Or imagine snuggling a **C**uddly **B**lue **R**accoon. While eating **C**reamy

Bacon **R**avioli. On a motorcycle. Whatever.

Commit

Everyone loves to fantasize, loves to wish. But few *commit.* For all the dreamers, he who commits and actually *does* is the exception.

If you're to fully and forever replace fanhood with manhood, you need to switch out of fantasy-pretend-cheerleader mode and into accomplishment-doer-achiever mode. Rather than wishing and wanting, today's the day you begin committing.

> "It would be so cool to be a skydiving instructor. What a life!"

> "I've always wanted to visit Germany in October. Wouldn't that be awesome?"

"I wish I had time to learn Brazilian Jiu Jitsu…"

Whatever your fantasies, if you've not been *doing* anything about them, now's the time. Harry Potter may have had adventures fall into his lap. But no Hagrid is going to break down our door and rescue us.

If you're going to make those adventures happen, committing – *really* committing – can't be a purely mental thing. If you leave the goal in your head, that's where it's likely to remain. But as life coach Brian Tracy teaches, we can outsmart our lazy, risk-averse subconscious by putting pen to paper.

You'll have doubts, worries, what-ifs. And writing your big goal down means you're serious this time, which means you might fail (oh no!). But pushing through this early hesitance is one price all doers must pay. Trust me, it's worth it.

This past weekend I watched a big boxing match on ESPN. Before my transformation the fight would have been a cool spectacle, but mysterious, foreign, scary. Now it feels like homecoming.

The athletes on TV are faster, tougher, fancier, and have better stamina than I ever did. But having trained and competed, I can relate. I can appreciate their angles and off-balance slips. I've weathered a barrage of punches, staved off a comeback, and mounted one of my own. I know what it feels like to take hard shots, to push through when my body's screaming stop,[25] and the primal joy of punching dudes in the face – the raw, undiluted satisfaction.

All else equal, I find dancing more enjoyable (works up a good sweat, is mentally stimulating, my nose doesn't get smashed). So I'm not here to convince you to abandon soccer for karate, Danielson. My point is simply that doing is far more enjoyable than wishing. In a phrase, *dreams are for suckers.* Or more precisely, dreams *that remain dreams* are for suckers.

No more wishing. No more fantasizing. You need concrete goals, a written commitment to pursue them,

---

[25] If you have fitness goals, know that your body is a liar. It'll tell you it can't when it definitely can. Don't give yourself a heart attack. But know that you're stronger than the flesh will admit.

and action. Now is the season of doing. So commit.

Begin

Just as soon as you commit, do something, anything, to move in the direction of accomplishing your big goal. This could be as simple as sending an email or making a phone call, visiting the courthouse or buying a suitcase, picking out running shoes or throwing out a box of donuts.

Tony Robbins considers acting boldly the core of any viable personal manifesto. It commits us to the path and builds momentum. It makes us instantly feel energized, enthused, *alive.* Plus, as David Schwartz put it:

"Action cures fear."

Whatever anxiety the mere thought of pursuing your adventure is causing (this is natural – I certainly felt it, and when I set new goals, like publishing potentially controversial books, still do), it will begin to dissolve as soon as you act decisively. Thinking and planning amplifies fear. Acting cures it.

At the outset of my combat arts adventure, the thing that most eased my mind was finally visiting the local boxing gym. And not simply watching, but jumping in and working out. Worrying over when I'd do it or what it would be like only made things worse and didn't bring me any closer to my destiny. But when I actually went, and especially when I did my first full boxer's workout (man, what a workout!), I started seeing myself as a fighter. I accepted the fact that I belonged in the ring just as much as anyone willing to put in the work.

After a couple of months of conditioning, the next step was slipping through the ropes for my first sparring session. It didn't go especially well. I mistook a padded jock strap for headgear (which means, yes, the sweaty jock part was draped over my face...). And when my coach corrected me ("That goes down here...") and I squared off against my first opponent, I looked more like "a moving punching bag," as one boxer friend put it, than a fighter.

It wasn't pretty. And it wasn't especially fun at first. But man, what a relief. All the pent up worry I'd been harboring, all the risks I'd blown out of proportion, I sweated out. Turns out I had a decent chin (against fitter, younger fighters with more muscle and skill, my chin was definitely tested).

But the more I sparred, the better I got. The better I got, the more comfortable I felt. Rather than simply eating shots, I started dishing them out. Pretty soon it was showtime for my first fight. Then my second. Then my third.

It's hard to explain how good that journey felt then, and how good recalling it feels now. I want you to experience that same satisfaction and pride.

There was a time I could have never imagined being comfortable in the ring. Today it just feels like home – in many ways, my happy place. (Remember Happy Gilmore's happy place, with the cowboy midget riding a stick horse and his grandma playing the one-armed bandit? No? Okay...) Action not only cures fear, sometimes it creates joy. And other times cowboy midget hallucinations.

As I said earlier, there's something primally satisfying about hitting dudes in the face – a life-changing thrill that I'd have never experienced had I not committed and taken those initial steps. At each stage of the journey, wondering and hoping and fretting – *thinking* about what I wanted and needed to do next – only added to the stress.

Ah, but when I *acted*, that's where progress began and fear ended.

I want the same for you. So remember, after you commit, don't wait. People who wait for conditions to be perfect before acting wait until they're dead. That's not you. Commit, then *begin*.

Research

At work and in life, I've seen so many spend so much time thinking rather than doing that I'm convinced some believe thinking *is* doing. That's why my method is commit, begin, *then* research – I don't want you to get stuck in the paralysis by analysis trap.

People will study and hem and haw until their window of opportunity has closed. Some seem to like it that way, I guess so they can avoid discomfort and the risk of failure.

But discomfort and the risk of failure, boys and girls, are the prices of success.

I got my ass handed to me when I first started boxing. This kid named Tristan hooked my temple so much that my head felt (and probably looked) like a speed bag. But I got better. Not better than Tristan. But good enough to hold my own against him, and good enough to get some sweet payback (mainly just stiff jabs, but stiff and frequent enough for me to feel good about our exchanges).

The point: we get this one life. *One.* Don't spend it planning and considering and deciding – hiding from uncertainty and discomfort when you could be winning. But at the same time, once you get going (and only once you get going – commit, begin, *then* research), figure out who's already blazed the path you're on and learn from them.

Whether your goal is to become a bowling champion, direct an after-school program, star in a play, become a NASCAR driver, launch a nonprofit, open a bakery – someone's already done it and written a good book on how.[26] Read that book and your path will not only be much easier, but your chances of success much higher.

When I was fighting I not only learned from my coaches and teammates, but from Smokin' Joe Frazier. His *Box Like the Pros* taught me

---

[26] Since you're reading right now, chances are good you already know this. But that there are good (intriguing, concise, practical, readable) books on how to do most anything was a huge revelation for me that didn't happen until my 20s. I had been too busy watching The Dukes of Hazzard and playing Atari (then Nintendo) for books (yuck!).

that a proper hook should feel like you're slamming a door (pivoting on the ball of your front foot, bent arm swinging your fist towards an opponent's temple, jaw or ribs).

A friend who had completed his own midlife crisis fighting challenge (which had doubled as post-divorce therapy) lent me fighter mindset books, Neuro Linguistic Programming books, and books on Jiu Jitsu technique and wrestling.

Spoiler: I didn't win the UFC welterweight division. But I was far more successful than I would have been without those resources. Without them, my modest fight record would certainly be worse, and I might have given up the first time Tristan rang my bell. With them, the adventure of a lifetime, a little success, and irreplaceable personal growth.

So find and apply the wisdom of those who've done your big thing already, but remain wary of man's tendency to ponder rather than do. I'm a philosopher by training, so I appreciate the value of a good ponder. But the truly wise man knows that while the unexamined life isn't worth living, the unlived life isn't worth examining.

No more indecision. No more delay. Transfer the excitement you used to feel for *their* season onto *your* season. Be your own marketing department, your own hype machine, your own coach with your own pre-game and halftime pep talks.

Nobody's going to do it for you. Accept that responsibility.

To get in the mood, look up "I am a champion speech" on YouTube, as well as anything by formerly homeless motivational speaker Eric Thomas. He's the guy your former heroes pay thousands to light a fire under their complacent asses. Let him light one under yours for free.

Chapter 18
Kenny Kool-Aids

As you distance yourself from your former team and start doing rather than cheering, friends and family will take notice. Some will be supportive. Some will not.

Some will take it personally, as might an alcoholic confronted by a drinking buddy who's decided to sober up. Changing suggests you think *they* need to change, too. And whether you're actually judging, this will stir inner conflict – remind them of whatever's driven them to fanhood and challenge their lifestyle. Some will respond by trying to drag you back down.

We'll call these people "Kenny Kool-Aids" after the Jonestown cultists who convinced one another that drinking poison was a good idea. Kenny Kool-Aids will say things like:

> "This is our year, I can feel it. C'mon, we've got a new coach. It's going to be great!"

or

> "Hey, I got tickets to the game. Join me? You know you want to..."

or

> "Quit being a prissy wimp and support the team. It's what men do!"

They might try to guilt trip you, reminding you of a family or group tradition. But once you tell them you're done, and especially when you explain why, they need to respect the decision. In case they don't (and some won't), be prepared to part ways. If they want to spend their time and money cheering for men of action rather than *being* men of action, that's their call. But you know better.

Remember Robert, the roommate who was with me during the end zone grass-pillaging '98 Florida game overtime win? The one who later named his son Neyland? We had a tradition of meeting up with a group of high school buddies for one UT home game per season. Even after he moved to Arizona and I (temporarily) moved to Baltimore/D.C., we made a point to travel in for that one annual bonding event.

When I first broke ties with the Vols, I was embarrassed to tell the crew. The team had been such an integral part of my identity for so long and had served as such a strong connection for us, I wasn't sure our friendship could evolve.

But I was sure that being true to myself was more important. The drummer boy incident had opened my eyes and I knew I needed to tackle my midlife crisis combat sports adventure before I got any older. Once I made the decision, there was no returning to a distracted life of mediocrity.

At first the guys didn't believe I was serious. I was usually the one pestering *them* to make it to the next game. I'd yell the loudest, act the wildest – the cheer captain of our annual reunion squad.

They assumed I'd come around once the team started winning again. But this wasn't a fair-weather thing. After the Vols eventually beat Florida, I still wasn't interested. I'd travelled too far down the path of manhood to ever absorb myself in fanhood again.

Eventually, the guys became cool with my decision. In fact, Robert concluded that breaking ties might really have been the best thing for me.

He told me, "I think you took it more seriously than I ever did."

This is questionable given that he's the guy who named his firstborn after a coach. But hey, if he's able to balance fanhood with manhood, that's fine with me. I'm here to help fans who want to change, not harass those who don't.

So it's okay to maintain friendships with old fanhood buddies. Just set clear boundaries and don't put up with any Kenny Kool-Aid bullshit.

If they choose to remain fans, that doesn't mean you can't be friends. It just means they have to respect your decision and that you'll have to find a new way to chill. Make it known that you value them, but that you need to take responsibility for your life and make it one actually worth living.

Regardless of how much they might push, I don't recommend calling them sissy cheerleaders – this would do more harm than good. Instead, try asking them whether the men they idolize are doers or cheerers.

> "Whose jersey do you think Peyton Manning snuggles up to at night?

That's right – Peyton doesn't live through other men. Neither should we."

The lesson: Don't follow sports stars. *Follow their example.*

Chapter 19
But, But, But...
Jack Nicholson

As you put down the pom-poms and pick up the skydiving goggles, running shoes, college books, coach's clipboard, shark food, etc., there's a negative voice in your head – your "bad wolf" – who's going to try to squash your ambition. He's going to whisper hypnotic lies, try to make you forget about SAP and CBR[27] and lull you back into precious, cheerleading sleep.

---

[27] Don't tell me you've forgotten the acronyms already... It's Scary Authentic Proud and Cuddly Blue Raccoon.

Your bad wolf will tell you there are plenty of successful sports fanatics out there, manly men, high achievers. If they can balance fanhood with a life fully lived, so can you.

> "Have you seen *The Departed? The Shining?* If the winner of three Academy Awards wants to let loose at Laker games, that doesn't make him any less of a man. I can be manly and fanly, just like Jack."

Are you Jack Nicholson? Neither am I.

But even if we were, every minute he's spent cheerleading is a minute he's not been doing something he wants, needs, or is afraid to do. Who knows what unfinished bucket list haunts the real Ed Cole. But I guarantee there's something. No man gets that absorbed unless he's running. Laker games are a distraction, and probably a frustrating distraction given the team's lackluster record of late.

The point is that even if you're curing cancer while managing an orphanage and perfecting biofuel, the problem with fanhood is that it ties a huge chunk of your identity to things beyond your control. Real men take credit for *their* accomplishments and responsibility for *their* mistakes. They don't whine about Brady's fumble or Harden's foul.

They don't strut around like they're the striker who hit the penalty kick that won the World Cup or sulk like they're the goalie who missed it. Real men reflect on their values, translate their dreams into goals, their goals into plans, and their plans into action. They don't simply wish or want. They pursue and accomplish. Their hands are too busy *doing* to shake pom-poms.

> "What about Spike Lee and the Nicks, Ice Cube and the Raiders, Jerry Seinfeld and the Yankees, Vladimir Putin and the St. Petersburg Zenit? Successful, manly men *and* fans."

When you're running Russia [insert your own Trump joke here], then we can talk. Until then, man up.

Pointing to successful sports fanatics is a bad wolf rationalization. Live your life, not theirs. We've been over this.

Chapter 20
But, But, But...
I'm Too Fat, Broke, Busy

Sometimes a deflected bad wolf will circle back and attack your flank. He'll shift from trying to convince you there's no need to change to trying to convince you you're too weak to change.

> "You don't have the time or the money. You're too old or too young, too tall or too short. Just watch the game – it's safer."

Have you heard of Nicholas Vujicic? The Australian born with Tetra-Amelia Syndrome? Instead of arms and legs, he got "flippers and stubs" (his words).

His occupation: motivational speaker and evangelist. His latest triumph: becoming a dad. Suck. It. Up.

Earlier I suggested that rather than worshiping athletes, you should consider becoming one yourself. And that if you physically couldn't, to give coaching a shot. Well, if we're going to talk about the motivational speaker without arms or legs, we need to talk about the football coach with the same condition.

Californian Rob Mendez grew up a 49ers fan. Passionate about football but unable to play, he decided to apply his mind to the game instead.

Volunteering as manager for his high school team, Rob studied the plays, the moves, the drills. He tested strategies on the Madden video game, then in real life, learning what worked and what didn't.

For 12 years he paid his dues as an assistant coach – running the quarterback drills from his wheelchair, drawing up plays on a whiteboard with a magic marker in his teeth. Then in 2018 he finally got his chance to be a head coach, entrusted with Prospect High School's junior varsity team.

A program that had been suffering losing seasons more often than not, Rob took his Panthers all the way to the West Valley JV League Championship. In his very first year. With no arms or legs.

They didn't win. But Rob was proud as ever of his team, his team proud as ever of him. And even though the loss hurt, you're not going to hear excuses or complaints.

> "Complaining is my No. 1 poison. So I try to stay positive. You hear stories about people with cancer, fighting for their lives. I'm fighting to have something to drink. To feel comfortable. So I try not to complain."[28]

Randy Pausch, author of *The Last Lecture*, is another remarkable person

---

[28] I stumbled upon Rob's SC Featured documentary, "Who Says I Can't," the Saturday morning it first aired in February, 2019. Thanks to producer Kristen Lappas for pursuing his story and to ESPN for airing it. Check out the video itself and Wayne Drehs's article, "Who Says I Can't," where the quote above is from, here: http://www.espn.com/espn/feature/story/_/id/25983010/who-says-rob-mendez-head-football-coach

without excuse or complaint. Diagnosed with pancreatic cancer and given six months to live, he decided to kick the rest of us in the pants with a seminar on how to achieve our childhood dreams.

Randy had dreamed of being a Disney Imagineer, so he worked to become their go-to virtual reality consultant. He'd always wanted to experience zero gravity, so he arranged to do it in NASA's astronaut training "vomit comet" jet. He'd fantasized playing in the NFL, and while he never did, he did negotiate a chance to practice with the Steelers.

Do you have arms and legs? Do you expect to live for more than six months?

That's what I thought. Whatever excuses your bad wolf is whispering, your life is too important, and Randy would emphasize *too short,* to listen. Nick knows you can do it. So does Rob. So suck it up and let's go.

Chapter 21
But, But, But...
It's My Outlet

"The one who watches athletic games instead of participating in athletics is involved in a surrogate achievement. But when you think about what people are actually undergoing in our civilization, you realize it's a very grim thing to be a modern human being. The drudgery... it's a life-extinguishing affair." – Joseph Campbell, *The Power of Myth*

Your job sucks, your girlfriend's mean, the specter of mortality haunts your existence. Stuck in a cubicle or on an assembly line, the season makes life's drudgery tolerable.

Or maybe you enjoy the serenity of a monk, yet resent having to be so *adult* all the time. Game time is the one time you can let loose. Bad behavior isn't just accepted, it's expected. And amongst the crowd, in body paint or dark enough sunglasses, you can play the anonymous adolescent, if only for a few hours.

I can relate. I rawed my vocal chords at many a big game. Mix one part SEC match-up with two parts Coke and one part Jack (or the other way around for some games) and this mild-mannered Southern gentleman became a bird-flipping game-day jackass. Yeehaw!

Self-loathing projected outwards? Reliving high school rebellion? Premature midlife angst? All I know is that big games released my inner jerk.

During one game I worked my way deep into the student section behind the Auburn bench, and when the stadium got just quiet enough, yelled:

> "Hey Cadillac Williams – *yo mama!*"

I'm not sure Williams, their star running back at the time, heard me, but his teammates sure did. They turned and looked, not with anger, but with confusion and pity.

> "Too much moonshine, hillbilly? Cadillac's an unpaid college athlete making something of himself. What are *you* doing, fanboy?"

The psychologists would say my "disinhibition" (more plainly, my "jackassery") was the result of the "deindividuation" I felt in a crowd of thousands of likeminded fans.[29]

Maybe that's true. But I'm sure I acted a fool in part because I had dreams and goals I was neglecting. How do I know?

Funny thing about finally becoming a fighter: I haven't had the urge to yell at an athlete, a television, or a drummer since.

I was initially tempted to simply transfer my fanaticism onto pro fighters – live through Anderson "The Spider"

---

[29] "The Psychology of Social Sports Fans: What Makes Them So Crazy?" by Thomas Van Schaik at SportsNetworker.com
http://www.sportsnetworker.com/2012/02/15/the-psychology-of-sports-fans-what-makes-them-so-crazy/

Silva or that "Triple G" boxer with the lightning punches. To punctuate my break from the Vols I hung a sign on my home office wall that read, "We are now UFC fans." Thankfully, instead of swapping one fanhood for another, I bought a mouthpiece and got to work.

Fighting was definitely tougher. Nobody ever got a concussion listening to Sports Talk, though some callers certainly sound like they've suffered a great deal of head trauma, and others like they're on the verge of a stroke. But actually competing confirmed its vast superiority.

One reason cheerleading can sometimes *feel* manly is that it triggers some of the same biological responses as competing. A 1998 study showed that when a fan's team wins, he receives a testosterone boost, as well as a testosterone dip when his team loses.

Author Eric Simmons attempted to replicate that study by taking saliva samples while watching his favorite hockey team, the San Jose Sharks.[30] His results were inconclusive, so he decided to research the physiological mystery further.

MRI tests showed that watching a buzzer-beater activates the same synaptic pathways as actually hitting the shot yourself. The effect is more intense for the athlete and more pronounced for fans who used to be players. But those vicarious thrills and chills you've had as a fan aren't simply in your mind – they're

---

[30] *The Secret Lives of Sports Fans: The Science of Sports Obsession.* Overlook Duckworth, Peter Mayer Publishers, Inc., 2013, page 21.

measurable in your physical brain as well.[31]

The chemical connection helps explain how we can get so swept up in the moment and why the escape has such a powerful attraction. As Simmons put it:

> "[P]art of the enjoyment of sports comes from surrendering your control and empowering your hormones and neurons to do their thing."[32]

Oddly enough, after intimate interviews with some of the most devoted fans of the historically worst teams, and after a thorough exploration of the psycho-physical forces driving the

---

[31] For more on mind/body dualism, google Descartes or take my Philosophy Intro.
[32] Ibid, page 93.

addiction, Simmons concluded that continuing fanhood is a smart choice.

I wrote this book for fans who want to let go, and have no desire to spoil the fun of fans who are content. If a guy can do fanhood in a healthy way, or if upon reflection he prefers the fantasy, that's his call. But let's be honest. It's a sad existence, we all deserve better, and we can all have better.

At the same time, I do get it. Spectator sports can be a welcome distraction, an outlet, a (superficial) way to connect with a tribe or simply a chance to hang with the guys. There's probably a warring instinct being satiated in there somewhere, too, and I'd rather repressed Germans cheer for their soccer team than invade Poland again.

So here's where I'll budge: I'm not saying you can't watch sports at all. When you first make the switch, do put distance between yourself and your old team. Do purge. After my awakening, I didn't watch the Vols for two years – no highlights, no web clips, nada. If they came on TV, I immediately changed the channel. If they were shown at a restaurant, we sat (or ate) somewhere else. The clean and total break was absolutely essential to my recovery.

But I did watch other teams (I said "watch" not cheer for) and I did study UFC and boxing matches since I was planning my run. The key is that I didn't associate with particular fighters, fight teams, or even fighting styles. I just observed the contest, briefly, then got back to living.

So it's OK to look forward to the season, generally, if you must. Watch some games (sometimes). Keep the basic ESPN package.

Just don't anchor your identity to any one team. Don't allow contrived rivalries in a made-up contest to supplant an authentic life fully lived. That's the unmanly part. That's the pathetic part. That's the shame, the waste.

If your addiction runs as deep as mine did, I recommend a complete break – both from your old team and also from that sport – for at least a season. No watching *just* the highlights, no listening to *just* a few minutes of sports talk, no reading *just* one article. Overcoming a serious addiction requires a serious commitment.

Going cold turkey will prove that you can thrive, find meaning and satisfaction without your former team. And once fully recovered, when you feel strong enough, there's nothing wrong with casually dabbling in spectating every now and again, though you may find you've developed such a disdain for fanhood that the appeal has completely vanished.

Chapter 22
Return to Neyland

September 23rd, 2017.

Today I attended my first UT football game in three years. The father of one of my son's best friends offered tickets last minute, and I reluctantly decided to give it a try.

On top of assuming the boys would have a good time, it was a test. After abstaining from anything remotely fan-like for a very long time, I claimed to be cured. I *felt* like I was cured. But was I?

Had it been a *Florida* game, I would have said no. While thickly scabbed over, that wound was still too tender.

But they were playing the University of Massachusetts, a non-conference buffer game designed to give the team a break between tougher opponents (like when Michigan schedules Appalachian State).

So Florida, no. Bama, no. But UMass? I could handle a UMass game. Surely.

I approached like Lieutenant Worf on a covert mission to Kronos.[33] Surrounded by clanmates who assumed I remained allegiant to the Klingon Emperor, returning to Neyland after the purge, after internalizing fanhood as cheerleading, after my crazy midlife

---

[33] Finally, the Star Trek references you've been waiting for.

crisis fight adventure, felt as sneaky as it did surreal.

A man in fan's clothing, detached from the outcome, for the first time I was able to simply observe.

The sound of familiar fight songs greeted us as we neared the entrances. So did a nine-foot statue of Coach Neyland – known as "General" Neyland for his service in the Army. A towering brick structure with flags along the top, the stadium felt a bit like his fortress.

As we reached our seats, I noticed the announcer praising the exceptional loyalty of Vol fans (suppress the risk of defection – check), the collective impact of their cheers (blur the boundary between spectator and competitor – check), and the storied history of the

Priiiiiiide of the Southland Marching Band (appeal to tradition – check).

References to "tradition" were everywhere, in fact – even at the concessions. Waiting in line for a snack, a sign read:

"UT football and Petros – *it's tradition.*"

Yes, the venerated tradition of chili, corn chips and Vol football – good to see the legend continuing in my absence.

I noticed pictures of Vol greats hung in the passageways, as well as former stars' retired #s by the scoreboards. Members of past teams were trotted onto the field between quarters to be honored (and gawked at), grainy replays from seasons gone by on the jumbotron. A gold star to the marketers for playing up the enduring legacy thing – making their research psychologist mentors proud.

Though most were civilized, I did see and hear (though fortunately didn't smell or feel) partially jovial, partially belligerent, drunks. One was hanging over the tunnel into Gate M telling everyone who walked underneath:

"I'm right here. Hey, I'm here!"

Okay, buddy – good for you. Four cops monitored the situation, making sure he stayed right there. I wondered how many times I had been that moron in someone else's eyes.

I have to admit it was a little sad. Excruciating heartbreaks aside, I had shared a great deal of joy in that place.

And I'd shared it with some special people at some special times: my dad when I was ten, my girlfriend (then wife) in my 20s, my son as a new dad, then with high school buddies for our annual mini-reunion.

Seeing the stadium on TV had been my connection to home when I was stuck in the desert, and Manning's greatness had been my personal redeemer when I was a lowly Airman. I didn't mention this before, but I actually flew in on leave in '97 to see him beat Texas Tech in the season opener, taking my two best friends from elementary school with me.

But my return after a three-year hiatus confirmed that the spell was broken. Despite the tug of nostalgia, I could finally see the spectacle for what it was – a manhood-robbing opiate for the misled.

Though I was passing the test, I was worried I might be sending my son mixed signals. He'd seen me at my worst (the television yelling, the mood swings) and had witnessed how difficult fanhood had been to shake in a culture where abandoning the team is viewed by many as traitorous. I'd risked friendships, even relationships with family members (the Vols remain a touchy subject for me and my sister).

I had explained why the hassle was worth it, and my son had agreed to help – always careful to refer to UT sports teams as "the Vols" rather than "Tennessee" so there would be no confusing strangers who play with balls with the beautiful state and people we continue to love. Kenny Chesney's "Back Where I Come From" still gives me chills. The same for Levon Helm's rendition of "Tennessee Jed." Ain't no place I'd rather be, either.

So why would a man who claimed to have released the childishness of fanhood (while reaffirming his love for home) take his son to a game? Had I been lying to him – to myself?

I was reassured when he was more interested in the campus library before the game and a museum after the game than what was happening on the field. Adults grouched about poor play calling and undisciplined corners. But the nine-year-olds had their priorities straight. Frolicking pregame in the library aisles, my son's friend exclaimed:

"I love this place!"

When the third quarter came, he led the petition to leave early. We were cooking in the sun, the game wasn't especially enjoyable (UMass was threatening a Wyoming-style upset) and the boys seemed to know that watching other men pursue their goals isn't nearly as worthwhile as doing something yourself, even if it's simply checking out a museum.

I was okay. Respectfully disengaged, but okay. There just wasn't anything there for me. The recovering alcoholic has little use for the bar. He can smell the codependency and wants no part of it. Sober and content, he can confidently resist. Such is the strength you'll enjoy once you've ditched fanhood for good.

Two weeks later, an Air Force buddy I hadn't seen in 20 years called out of the blue. Both of us country boys from the Volunteer state, we'd been best friends during boot camp, enduring a drill sergeant affectionately nicknamed "Satan." Now working as a park ranger near Nashville, he'd found me online and had tickets to the South Carolina game, understandably assuming I'd be interested. I was interested in seeing him, but not the team.

I mentioned the drummer boy incident and explained that as a result I'd distanced myself from the program, but didn't have the heart to discourage him further. Eager to see an old pal (my best pal during those trying first weeks in the military), I agreed to return to Neyland a second time.

Was this the beginning of a pattern? Was I genuinely cured?

Once again, I was pleasantly immune, even better able to observe the marketing schemes along with the fans' responses to it.

I tried not to look down my nose at anyone. How could I? Society tells us it's normal, even macho to be a rabid fan. When life sucks, it's an effective distraction, a way to *feel* like you're accomplishing something when we're really not. And the drama, the thrills, the shared euphoria – grown men can openly express emotions in the context of fanhood we're otherwise expected to suppress. For those reasons and more, fanhood is possibly the most common form of self-medication, even when the side-effects ultimately outweigh the benefits.

So I got it. I still get it. But that doesn't make it any less of a sissified waste.

As they had done so many times before, the team lost a last-minute heartbreaker. My Air Force buddy didn't seem too upset. Perhaps seeing me dissociated inspired him to rethink his own fanhood. But I didn't push it. He'll have to come to that conclusion on his own.

Watching friends and family go overboard as fans can be tough. But preaching about how silly it is would only drive them away. Instead, lead by example.

Sooner or later, those with the potential to come around will. Nudge gently, if you nudge at all, and trust that your living rather than cheering will inspire them to do the same.

I know fanhood feels safer than living. I know the industry makes it look cool. I know friends and family are going to challenge your loyalty, tempt you with free tickets, even try to trick you into watching ("Hey, we're having a get-together Saturday at the same time as kickoff... no special reason... Join us?"). Trust me, I know.

But you've been down that dead end. You know it's a profit-driven ruse – the slow motion, the flags, the pageantry – all ploys to make fanhood seem more meaningful than it is. And you know that you deserve and can have better.

Whether your (former) team is on the winning or losing end of a streak, don't let their performance affect your self-perception. You didn't do jack to help the wins and you didn't do jack to cause the losses. Find meaning in *your* record, and make it a record your 85-year-old self can be proud of.

It's taken some heavy-duty brainwashing to convince us that second-rate cheerleading is worthwhile, and powerful, profit-hungry forces (backed by brilliant, albeit ethically suspect psychologists) want to keep it that way. So it's going to take some heavy-duty deprogramming to escape. I hope associating fanhood with cheerleading has been as compelling a motivator for you as it was for me.

Whatever adventures you've been neglecting, finally tackling them is going to be far more fun and fulfilling than the mediocrity of fanhood could ever be.

So purge your old gear (in a box to the garage or back of the closet *now)* and make that list of what you've accomplished in the last five, ten years to contrast with the team. Whether you've underperformed or outperformed those strangers, what's the scary, cool thing you've been avoiding – the one that feels authentic, and that you envision being proud of on the other side?

Whatever that is for you, commit (put pen to paper), begin (taking action *now* is the most important step), and research (someone's already done it – find and apply their wisdom). Comfort zone expansion is a beautiful thing, and easier when you're riding a Honda CBR or snuggling a Cuddly Blue Raccoon.

If I could box for the first time at 37, you can do your cool thing, too. So what are you waiting for? Trash the skirt. Fanhood to manhood. Let's go!

If you enjoyed *Fanhood to Manhood,* tell a friend or leave a brief review on Amazon. Doesn't have to be fancy.

Thousands are just as brainwashed as we were, and have no idea there's a cure. If we don't tell them, who? But then purge and get on with it – let's go.

Cheers,
"Tommy"

More Books by "Tommy Knoxville"

Year of the Fighter:
Lessons from my Midlife Crisis Adventure (2018)

⭐⭐⭐⭐⭐ 44 ratings

What it felt like to step in the ring for the first time, to do it against fighters half my age, and to sometimes win. The joys of getting kicked in the face, of being so exhausted (and possibly concussed) that I puked, and the self-coaching it took to make a lifelong dream a reality.

Friends made, relationships affirmed, values clarified, childhood vindicated, midlife crisis conquered (whew!). Plus there's a whole section on the SAP and CBR stuff, with examples tied back to my fight experience. So if an inside look at my crazy adventure might help you tackle yours, check it out. Especially enjoyable if you've ever fantasized becoming Rocky, enjoy a good UFC, or like that Cobra Kai show.

The Best Public Speaking Book
2nd Edition (2019)

★★★★★ ˅   30 ratings

Avoid public speaking? Cringe your way through it when forced? We can fix that.

First, there's an "Urban Honey Badger" assertiveness drill (that's an urban honey badger on the cover), scientifically proven to boost stage presence and thicken chest hair. Learn how to organize your messages so they're easy to remember and deliver. Discover and polish your authentic stage self. Don't simply *survive* on stage. Decide to *dominate*.

Based on my experience going from terrified rookie to conference presenter, paid keynote speaker and comedy club host, as well as years coaching students in my oral-concentration philosophy classes. The core: *Know Thy Material, Be Thyself and Practice.*

Recommended Reads

The Miracle Morning by Hal Elrod

Arnold Schwarzenegger's advice for finding time to pursue your dreams: "Sleep faster."

Whether you get eight hours or four, Elrod's *Miracle Morning* will show you how to begin your day energized and fulfilled. My custom routine inspired by his advice: 30 minutes of reading on the elliptical (exercising the mind and body at the same time – best multitasking I do all day), 10 minutes of journaling while brewing coffee (sometimes black tea), followed by 10 minutes of semi-guided meditation (if you're new to meditating, check out the *Calm* app's free trial).

Some mornings my bad wolf convinces me to hit snooze. But on my better days, this is a first hour well spent. See Elrod's tips on developing your own.

The War of Art by Steven Pressfield

For creative types (like me), this concise gem names the negative voice haunting all artists: *Resistance,* and shows us how to defeat him.

The doubts, the worries, the self-sabotage – every human who's attempted to produce something original has had to deal. Homer and Hank Jr. battled the same demons that are smothering your genius. Pressfield shows us how to persevere.

This Year I Will by M. J. Ryan

One of the best goal accomplishment books written. Mixed with *The Miracle Morning*, *The War of Art* and CBR, a recipe for badassery.

The 7 Habits of Highly Effective People by Stephen Covey

Begin with the end in mind, insist on win-wins, spend your time doing things that are important but not urgent – these are the habits of winners. A best-selling classic for a reason. And for couples and parents, his *7 Habits of Highly Effective Families* is superb.

The Magic of Thinking Big by David Schwartz

This is the guy who gave me the "action cures fear" insight. A second favorite concept: "the crippling disease of *excusitis.*" Also available in a well-produced audiobook, it's a tad corny, but I'm the dude pushing the SAP acronym, so who am I to judge.

The One Thing by Gary Keller

Achieving anything of value requires focused chunks of time. So prioritize what matters and hammer away until they're complete. You have Gary's (and my) permission to leave the unimportant stuff undone. (And see Covey's 7 Habits for clarity on what's important and what isn't.)

Eat That Frog by Brian Tracy (actually, anything by Brian Tracy)

If you had to eat a frog, would you stretch it out for hours, nibble by nibble, or would you just swallow it in two quick gulps? Such is Tracy's approach to getting things done.

The unpleasant stuff you have to do, knock it out first and fast, and the rest is cake. And if you don't want to read the book, there's a nice abridged audio version as well.

Finish: Give Yourself the Gift of Done by Jon Acuff

Good at starting stuff but not finishing? Acuff shows us how to conquer perfectionism and actually finish what we've started.

A favorite insight: "Goals you refuse to chase don't disappear—they become ghosts that haunt you. Do you know why strangers rage at each other online and are so quick to be angry and offended these days? Because their passion has no other outlet."

Remember how I lost the desire to yell at the TV once I pursued my fight dream? Yep. Give your passion some sunlight and you'll mellow a bit, too.

Acknowledgements

Thanks to my wife and kids for putting up with me when I was a rabid fan and for supporting me during my transition. I continue to be a work in progress – thank you for your love and patience.

Sports fanaticism borders on the religious where I come from, and breaking ties with the local team was a cardinal sin in many people's eyes. So thanks to the friends and family who've overlooked my heresy and stuck by me. I suppose we'll find out who's left once this book is published!

Thanks to my original editor, Debi Stansil, for your careful read, review, suggestions, and coaching. If not for your insight and suggestion, *Fanhood to Manhood* would be a mere section of *Year of the Fighter.* They're definitely better as standalone books. Also, a note to the grammaticians that you sternly reminded me that "dragged" is the proper past-tense version of "drag," and not "drug." I take full responsibility for that, and all instances of improper colloquialisms. Southerners say "drug" and "ain't." Ya'll know what we mean.

Equal thanks to my second editor, Eric Wyman (joining the

project a year after Debi), who also tried to convince me to change drug to dragged, but was insistent that I be more authentic. I'm glad you convinced me to print "pussy" rather than "puss," "asshole" rather than "jerk," and "shit" rather than nothing at all, even though my well-mannered ten-year-old tried to convince me to do the opposite (bless his heart).

Thanks to "Colonel" Gary Taft for reviewing an early draft and encouraging me to both bolster the psychological research section (which was virtually nonexistent when he read it) and to consider toning down the skirt/cheerleader stuff. I realized that stuff could be perceived as insensitive and offensive, both to actual cheerleaders, and possibly women in general. So when editor #2 Eric had the same reaction, on his advice I rewrote the intro to explain and defend the approach, and took pains to clarify that while there's nothing wrong with being a cheerleader, sports fans are falsely portrayed as edgy contributors.

My goal was to simply destroy that myth for the sake of my target audience – victims of toxic fanhood eager to change. Whether that approach proved best, we'll see. But I'm certain readers will benefit from the psych research chapter, so many thanks for pushing me to write it.

And finally, thanks to all the coaches and teammates who helped me thrive during my own transition. I was such a ridiculous sports fan in part because I had been suppressing my fight dream. Actually living it is something for which I'll be forever proud. And I couldn't have done it without the support of many – Jesse, Poke, Jamey, Mr. Ogle, Matt, Buck, Scott, Mario, and Stephen at the top of the list.

Thank you, brothers. And of course, thanks to my wife for picking up my slack at home while I was busy getting punched in the face, and to my kids for excusing my absences, not getting too freaked out by my black eyes, and for always being in my corner.

P.S. I'm releasing all my titles on audiobook in 2021 (one of my goals for the year), including this one. So if you like listening or know someone who would benefit from the message but treats books like kryptonite, check Audible soon.

Cheers, *"Tommy"*

www.ingramcontent.com/pod-product-compliance
Lightning Source LLC
Chambersburg PA
CBHW030439300426
44112CB00009B/1073